Language is a remarkably powerful instrument for affecting personal change. I discovered years ago, as an undergraduate student, that spoken language can assist an individual to make cognitive leaps that traditional "talk" therapies often cannot. Such applications of language, when used intentionally to pace then lead a person into their own internal experience of change, can be almost magical!

The written word can be just as powerful. Because Steve writes with a disarming and unassuming style, he invites the reader to explore with him places that are scary and painful. Because he is talking about himself, it can feel safe for a victim of severe stress trauma to follow the narrative while reliving his or her own experience at various levels of consciousness. (Most cognitive-behavioral approaches to treatment of PTSD require this "reliving" step as part of the therapeutic process.) He also leads the reader who is in denial or who has sublimated the painful experiences so deeply that they are no longer conscious, through a series of self-identifying symptom descriptions. Again, because Steve is only talking about himself and members of his family, readers can absorb as much or as little of the information as they are ready to. Finally, using his self-effacing but tremendously insightful style, he draws the reader through actual transformative therapeutic processes that support healing and lead to more constructive means of coping.

This is a book that will get a great deal of attention for many years to come!

—Byron Lewis, M.A., author of *Magic of NLP Demystified:*
A Pragmatic Guide to Communication and Change

Reconciliation: A Son's Story, takes us on a dark, painful journey, through intergenerational PTSD and the broken lives it leaves behind. In the end, the author gives us hope, as he confronts his own PTSD, and works through it. He shows us the way back is through forgiveness, redemption, education, and unconditional love. The author's story is unique and yet it isn't. Approximately 8 Million Americans will experience PTSD at some point in their lives. Steve has the courage to share his story, hoping it will help others to address their PTSD and break the intergenerational cycle. I encourage anyone who suspects they or someone they love may have PTSD, to seek help from a Licensed Therapist.

The author includes a short self quiz to help the reader identify if they are at risk. He also includes a layperson's assessment as a starting point for self discovery. Don't go the journey alone. As in Steve's story, it requires connectedness with others to go down the path of hope and healing.

—Beverly Ventura, Marriage Family Therapist and Life Coach
Lagunacounseling.com

YO-BRV-007

PUBLISHER'S NOTE

Every once in a while as a publisher, I come across that rare manuscript that I just think every one should read. Steve Sparks' book, *Reconciliation: A Son's Story*, is one of those. This is an American story about an American father who went to war and came back changed by what he saw and by what he experienced. How this impacted his family was profound, yet unrecognized for what it was back then. Today we know much more about the effects of Post Traumatic Stress Disorder (PTSD) on the individual, but what about the family members closest to that person? Steve Sparks explores this in a compelling way that helps all of us to not only better understand this topic, but also appreciate the sacrifices that our war verterans and their families have made for our nation. An American story...

John McClure
Signalman Publishing
Kissimmee, Florida
October, 2011

Rocky

DEC 29, 2012

Reconciliation

A Son's Story

this story is About
Forgiveness & Spiritual
Healing.

Steve Sparks

Reconciliation: A Son's Story
by Steve Sparks

Signalman Publishing   2011
www.signalmanpublishing.com
email: info@signalmanpublishing.com
Kissimmee, Florida

© Copyright 2011 by Stephen H. Sparks. All rights reserved. No part of this book may be reproduced or transmitted in any form or by any means, electronic or mechanical, or incorporated into any information retrieval system, electronic or mechanical, without the written permission of the copyright owner.

Cover design by Lisa Thomson

ISBN: 978-1-935991-30-4 (paperback)
          978-1-935991-31-1 (ebook)

Library of Congress Control Number: 2011939588

Signalman
Publishing

This book is dedicated to my three daughters, Deanna, Bianca, and Sarah. Each has had their own life experiences and challenges, which helped me profoundly in writing the story. I love them with all my heart, and hope this story provides answers to many questions that have gone unanswered in the past. I also hope this story provides future generations a perspective of the Sparks' family that until now has not been articulated effectively. It is even more important that this story offers a learning experience that enables each of my loving daughters to achieve peace in their own lives.

In Memory:

*Vernon H. Sparks (1918-1998), BMC United States Navy,
World War II and Korean War*

Combat veteran who served his country with pride and honor

In honor of

all Veterans and loved ones

November, 2011

Contents

Foreword

In March, 2011, my husband and I traveled to Bucerias, Mexico. Our first night there we met the woman in the room next to us while sitting outside on our patio. As the woman said good bye, she casually mentioned her husband would be reliving another helicopter battle in Vietnam that evening and hoped we would not be disturbed. I asked if he was okay and she said he suffered from Post Traumatic Stress Disorder, and relived the dream night after night. We met her husband in the elevator the next day; he was a gentle, quiet man. From outward appearances we would never have known he suffered from a mental health issue. After our weekend we upgraded to a larger suite in an adjacent building and did not run into our neighbors again before their departure from the resort.

Steve had started documenting his father's World War II history about two months prior to our trip. He planned to request his father's naval records when we returned from Mexico. As luck would have it, about six days into our trip I became ill and dehydrated, and more or less completely missed two days of our Mexican adventure. Being a devoted, caring husband, Steve stayed in the room with me while I recovered from a vicious bacterial infection. While I slept, he worked on his "story" to record his family history for our children and grandchildren. Having a clear head away from our daily grind, his "story" began evolving into something much larger.

As I read this body of work I began to see the story as a case study from the perspective of a lay person. Steve had shared some of his childhood memories with me, but as he embraced each of his siblings in telling their stories, I saw a much bigger picture unfolding. Steve's new awareness about his father's "battle fatigue" condition of the past became the catalyst for a significant self-discovery journey. My husband's journey through dark moments of his past created an opportunity to lift an invisible veil that both of us had not really fully acknowledged. The value of facing the truth has been powerful and healing.

Over the last 28 years that I've been with my husband I have felt he was misunderstood more than not. It is clear to me now that misunderstandings are often not the fault of anyone, but the result of not having all the information and communication barriers. Maybe I'm the exception, not the rule, in separating some of the behaviors from the man I fell in love with. I am hopeful that those closest to him see a more complete picture of who he is, and his hopes and dreams for his loved ones. Steve has a warm heart and a loving spirit; writing this story makes it even more apparent.

Watching my anxious partner embrace a more peaceful and happy existence has been a positive journey for me as well. I have a much greater understanding of what his life has been about during times of struggle. I don't believe much in coincidences. My philosophy has always been that life experiences unfold as they were meant to be. The timing of Steve's writing journey is part of the greater plan. He is able to embrace the truth, learn from this experience and share that with those he loves deeply. His motivation has also been to help others who may have experienced family trauma, especially related to military service. He wants to share his newfound peace and hopefully make a difference for the greater good.

I've often thought about the couple next door in Mexico during these last months. Steve's extensive research on PTSD has given me an informed perspective I did not have previously. My hope is that our short time neighbors in Mexico and other war veterans are able to reach a peaceful existence within their own families, and break the cycle of intergenerational PTSD. Although there are many take-aways in Part 3 of this book for all to consider, perhaps the greatest is knowing that none of us is alone in our life's journey. Unconditional love exists for each of us from a higher power or, if we're fortunate enough, from earthly family and friends as well. In love lies our strength.

Judy Young Sparks
Depoe Bay, Oregon
September, 2011

Acknowledgments

I could not have written *Reconciliation, a Son's Story* without the help and support of family and friends, especially my loving wife, Judy Young Sparks. Judy kept my spirits up all through this most amazing journey. She encouraged me during times when the research was painful, and cheered me on as the writing progressed, sometimes in high energy brain dumps. Writing is definitely a joy for me, but it takes a team. Following are others who played key roles helping me with the story.

- Bianca Cavello – my loving daughter started me thinking in late 2010 with her question about knowing me better and not knowing very much about my family as a whole. This really got my attention, so writing this story is my way of responding. She also contributed a very eloquent and moving quote in the book about "unconditional love."

- Sarah Sparks – my youngest and dear daughter was consistently encouraging and provided some of her own thoughts and ideas when she was home from school on weekends. She was close to earning her degree in psychology from the University of Oregon when writing this story was a big topic of discussion at home.

- Deanna Sparks – the oldest of my three daughters is very special. Her wisdom and insight from her own life experiences helped me considerably, especially during our visit in the summer of 2011. She has overcome her own major life challenges as a single mother of two children.

- Beverly Ventura – a dear friend who left the information technology (IT) business and became a therapist. Bev gave me the initial "green light" when she read my early draft while the story was just beginning to take shape. She has continued to encourage and help me throughout this process, especially as it relates to the clinical aspects of Post Traumatic Stress Disorder (PTSD). Thanks to Bev's encouragement and support, I finally started to believe that my gift of writing and passion could make a difference on a very important subject and contemporary issue.

- Byron Lewis – My best friend in retirement and neighbor helped review my work along the way. His compassion and generosity along with his own expertise in the field of psychology and life experiences were extremely valuable. Byron also authored and published, *Magic of NLP Demystified: A Pragmatic Guide to Communication and Change*, Byron A. Lewis and R. Frank Pucelik, Metamorphous Press, Lake Oswego, OR, 1982 and *Sobriety Demystified: Getting Clean and Sober with NLP and CBT*, Byron A. Lewis, M.A., Kelsey & Co. Publishing, Santa Cruz, CA, 1996

- Jack Brown – My close friend and mentor helped me realize that writing about my father would bring me closer to forgiveness and healing. He helped me believe that sharing my Dad's experience in WWII would go a long way to help many others in the same ways it has helped me.

- Jerry Sparks – My oldest brother really had to step up and revisit his own pain from the past to help me with the story. I could not have written the truth without my dear brother's help and support. He is a retired US Navy Warrant officer who served his country with honor and distinction for 30 years, including the Vietnam War.

- Dan Sparks – My younger brother helped me remember many events of the past. His assistance allowed me to maintain the authenticity of our family's story. He also contributed the idea of the "Me, I, Culture" in Part 3 of this book.

- Laura Sparks – My younger and loving sister who suffered for many years living in a toxic home and in transforming and healing herself in adult life, also helped me to remember events that could not have been accurately written without her help. Laura's perspective on the feelings of women was especially helpful in understanding our mother better.

- Scott Sparks – My youngest brother's help was most significant since he lived in a different generation as a sibling with all his older brothers gone. He was also able to relate his own experiences in adult life and healing from being exposed to a toxic home culture. Scott served in the U.S. Air Force.

- Marcella Sparks – Last but not least, my dear Mother, at age 93, was a huge help in connecting the dots on so many things that were difficult to understand or remember. Mother endured a life of significant personal challenges as a wife of a WWII combat veteran and survivor of the Depression era.

- United States Navy – I could not have pieced together my Dad, Vernon's WWII record, including medical condition, if his entire naval record was not available to family members. The Navy has excellent archives accessed via websites that were extremely helpful in capturing WWII during Pearl Harbor and the Asiatic Pacific Theater, including the USS West Virginia and USS Belle Grove where Dad served during the worst parts of WWII in the Pacific.

- USS Belle Grove Association – The best discovery of my research produced two living shipmates from the USS Belle Grove's war cruise in the Asiatic Pacific Theater along with several photos that were critical to my research.

- Cliff Viereck – A surviving shipmate from the USS Belle Grove who sent me crew photos from the time and the ship's war cruise map referenced in the story. Cliff also provided his own account of living aboard the USS Belle Grove and one of seven campaigns, the taking of Iwo Jima. I took the liberty to edit his account as an interview so that it could be included in my story. I know Mr. Viereck will be pleased to see how his story was used in the context of the USS Belle Grove war cruise and the Asiatic Pacific Theater during WWII. Mr. Viereck had his own account of the experience published in the USS Belle Grove Association newsletter. Cliff was 17 years old when he joined the Navy in 1943.

- Charlie Minter – A surviving shipmate who knew Dad well during the USS Belle Grove war cruise sent me an e-mail describing "Bosn Sparks" as a salty Chief Petty Officer (CPO) and leader. It was a very emotional experience to read about my father from this time so long ago. Charlie was 17 years old when he joined the Navy in 1943.

- Rear Admiral Mike McCaffrey – It made a huge difference in the story talking about my Dad's personality and style at home as a father by including Admiral McCaffrey's humorous and poetic description of a salty Chief Petty Officer.

- F. Magdalene Austin, Sun Drip Journals – A highly talented artist who uses her unique and beautiful art as healing therapy. My story includes a quote from Ms. Austin about the value of "reaching out."

- Andy Feola – A retired educator who reinforced the need for a writer to be prepared to "judge themselves first" to maintain authenticity.

- Steve Power – a friend and photographer who employs a new Nikon product developed by NIX, Capture NX2. The tool allows the selection of an area in a photograph adds or subtracts brightness and contrast, sharpness or blur. The technology is especially effective with old photographs.

- Neighbors for Kids (NFK) – Provided me with the personal and professional space to develop a free and open mind to explore new horizons in my life at a time when high energy and passion were critical in writing this story. NFK is a non-profit youth after-school program, including academics, recreation, and mentor support. www.neighborsforkids.org

Introduction

Vernon H. Sparks, BMC, U.S. Navy (1918 – 1998)

This story is written to honor my father's sacrifice to his country during WWII, Korean Wars, and as a survivor during the attack on Pearl Harbor, December 7, 1941. The story will also show how battle affected the lives of the men who experienced extreme trauma to body and mind at a time when mental health research and treatment were barely getting attention. This story is also about the families who were affected by the war, who suffered and sacrificed during the war and long after with the symptoms of Post Traumatic Stress Disorder (PTSD).

Sparks, Vernon H, b. 12/10/1918, d. 02/27/1998, US Navy, BMC, Res: Orangevale, CA, Plot: C-4 0 42, bur. 04/21/1998 http://files.usgwarchives. net/nv/lyon/cemeteries/fernleys.txt

USS West Virginia (BB-48) prior to its sinking during the Japanese attack on Pearl Harbor, December 7, 1941 (U.S. Navy photograph).

Marcella C. (Schaub) Sparks   **Vernon H. Sparks**

Remember Pearl Harbor Plaque

Americans supported the war effort in numerous ways. Gladys Grabinski - the mother of Louis Grabinski, who served aboard the West Virginia - hung this plaque in her kitchen from 1942 until the end of the war:

Postcard of Dad's first duty station, USS Tennessee, following boot camp in 1936.

PART I

HISTORY

I regret deeply not attending my father's memorial service in 1998. I was angry, very angry for a long time. Dad was sick from his WWII experience during my childhood. As a family, we experienced significant physical and mental abuse for many years. He was an alcoholic for most of his adult life, treating his demons with a substance that was never healing and served only to bring him and his family down. Post Traumatic Stress Disorder (PTSD) was not well understood during those years as it is now, so alcohol was the chosen medication. The men who served in the military during WWII were too proud to express their pain objectively or to admit a need for treatment, including living in a culture that would not listen anyway. We survived our childhood and became successful, but not without baggage and our own severe emotional challenges in life. My mother, Marcella, survived too, remarkably well considering what she endured. At the time of this writing, Mother was just turning 93 living in Reno, Nevada, surrounded by the best care and a loving family. But this story is not about me or any other member of the family, it is about how the legacy of war affects those who are not in the fight directly, the family members and loved ones of emotionally wounded veterans of WWII and all wars. This story is certainly about a hero from the "Greatest Generation" of men and women who sacrificed dearly to protect our freedoms and liberties during a terrible period in the history of the United States of America.

Battleship USS West Virginia

From Ship's Crew Muster:
Sparks, Vernon H.   *328-41-29 Cox. 13 Jan. 36 10/12/39*

On the morning of December 7, 1941, Dad was on duty as a coxswain aboard the USS West Virginia ("WeeVee") anchored in Pearl Harbor, Hawaii. Close to 8am that beautiful Sunday morning he heard explosions and immediately looked out open portholes along with a fellow seaman. My dad watched in horror as his shipmate's head was blown off just a few

1

feet from him. He watched in disbelief as his shipmate fell backward to the deck without his head attached. The battle stations alarm sounded and shortly after the "abandon ship" call came. Dad, along with many other shipmates, jumped ship into an inferno of fire from burning oil. While trying to save others and suffering burns, he swam to Ford Island where he was met by Marines who took him to a safe location for treatment of his wounds. And this experience was just a warm-up to the worst that would come later as the war in the Pacific unfolded after the United States declared war on Japan.

"Almost immediately, the *USS Oklahoma* and *USS West Virginia* began taking deadly hits. The mighty battleships shook violently as torpedoes slammed into their hulls, ripping metal as if it were tinfoil. Water rushed through the gaping wounds in their sides and oil spread outward on the surface of the harbor. Bombs continued to fall, striking the other big ships moored beside the *West Virginia* and *Oklahoma*. The oil on the surface of the water ignited to send towering pillars of smoke into the blue morning skies." (http://www.homeofheroes. com/pearlharbor/pearl_4fire.html)

The Japanese used 354 planes to torpedo, dive bomb, horizontal bomb, and strafe ships and air bases. All but 28 returned safely to their aircraft carriers and were available to participate in the Battle of Midway five months later. According to Navy reports of the event, it was a complete and total surprise, a surreal experience. No one could believe that any country in the world would even think of attacking the United States of America's Naval Fleet.

It gives me pause to think about this "surreal" event in the minds of men who were mentally unprepared for the attack. I can imagine when the first explosions were heard that one would not make a connection to torpedoes or bombs being delivered precisely to their targets with the intent to surprise, destroy, and kill in what was considered a "safe harbor." Looking out "open portholes" during an attack or even having the portholes open was neither an acceptable practice nor how sailors were trained to respond.

Watching a fellow seaman get his head literally blown off his shoulders would create a shock to the body and mind that would forever be implanted in a person's psyche. This surprise attack had to be an "Armageddon" for those either with religious or non-religious beliefs. How would any of them who survived get the experience rationalized to the extent that they could go on to fight another day? How would their lives be affected, and how could they even discuss the event with family members who would not understand? Would they decide not to discuss it at all? We now know the answer and subsequently became victims as family members and paid a price ourselves, but not even close to the price our dear heroes and my father paid.

After the USS West Virginia

Dad was reassigned to Shore Patrol in Hawaii following the attack. He was able to come home between the time on Shore Patrol and being assigned to the newly commissioned USS Belle Grove (LSD-2) on August 9, 1943. My mother really didn't know if he was dead or alive for quite some time. He was not home when his first son, Jerry, was born prior to the Pearl Harbor invasion, and did not see his son until he was around 16 months old. Dad really didn't have the chance to know him at all until the end of WWII in 1945. My brother would often say it was difficult to know Dad, and he was scary. We all found out what he was talking about as we came into the world and began to observe and experience our father's sickness ourselves. The war really took its toll on Dad along with thousands of other sailors and soldiers of that period. It is important to spend some quality time on my father's history prior to moving on to the remainder of his experience in WWII serving on the USS Belle Grove (LSD-2) in the Asiatic Pacific Theater. Who was this young man who joined the Navy at age 17? What was he all about before experiencing the ravages of war?

Vernon H. Sparks History

Vernon H. Sparks was born in Eldred, Minnesota on December 10, 1918, to Art and Mildred Sparks, a poor family from North Dakota. The family resided in the St. Paul area while he spent his younger years attending school and working whenever he could to help his family survive the depression years. Dad joined the Navy as soon as he turned 17. It was the only opportunity for him at the time, and it was his dream to serve in the military, especially to "join the Navy and see the world" as the advertising promoted at the time.

My dad talked fondly of his childhood, especially times on his grandparents farm in the Red River Valley in North Dakota. He loved this time as a child the best. His grandmother, Mattie, was a Lakota Sioux Native American, and his grandfather, Aaron McClellan Sparks' family was from Ohio. Aaron's uncle was George Brinton McClellan (1826-1885), a Philadelphia native of Civil War and Union Army fame, according to Sparks family ancestry records (ref. McClellan, http://www.civilwarhome.com/macbio.htm). For a long time having Native American blood lines was shameful for families. I'm told by those knowledgeable of the history, that even the Lakota wanted to hide the fact because they were knocked down so much by the Catholic Christian movement at the time that they felt their heritage was less than human and evil. I find this apparent fact despicable! I feel so proud to have just 1/16 Lakota in my blood. I believe Native Americans were treated even worse than our African American brothers and sisters. Native Americans were already here and owned the sacred land, and we must have mown them over like animals and orchestrated a sort of genocide to remove these special peoples from our new Christian society and culture. I will do everything I can to ensure that my family has full and complete information on our proud Native American heritage.

Dad rode horses, hunted, fished, and worked hard. His grandparents were highly respected and well off at the time. Their three sons, including my grandfather Art, all had their life challenges and success eluded them for the most part, except for Uncle Harry, who took his inheritance and bought a farm in Ascov, Minnesota. Uncle Bob Sparks was alone and mostly homeless when he committed suicide by hanging himself in Chicago around 1957. Grandpa Art passed away in his mid 60's of a heart condition and alcoholism, basically a poor and unhappy man. My grandmother Mildred lived well into her 80's and had mostly close relationships with her children and grandchildren. There was one daughter, Ruth and husband, Alex who we met while in Minnesota. I don't remember Ruth's married name. Ruth and Alex had twin sons and one daughter according to my Mother, Marcella. Brother, Danny, told me we lived with Ruth and Alex for a short time when we moved to Minnesota, but my memory fails me again. I didn't see much of any of them after joining the Navy, but recently have reconnected with my cousins and surviving aunts while doing research for this story.

My daughter, Bianca, and her family at the time of this writing moved to Eden Prairie, Minnesota, giving me more motivation to find my way back and to share family roots with Bianca and grandkids, Joey and Jordan. Another effect of my own PTSD condition was to ignore where my family lived and my roots, sharing hardly anything with my children until recently. Discussions about my own parents have been limited to negative references for the most part, leaving my kids with a feeling that they didn't want anything to do with my family. I take full responsibility for this behavior, and intend to make amends by writing this story and sharing my family history with my own family for the rest of my time.

Until writing this story, I didn't take the time to know my parents when they were married and before the war. To begin with it is important to understand Vernon H. Sparks, the person and man before WWII and years of combat duty that took its toll on his mind and body. What was Dad like? I took a chance and asked Mother, knowing that she is almost 93 and not articulate nor with the best memory at this time in her life.

While talking to Mother on July 25, 2011, I was able to ask her a few questions about her observations of Dad's behavior prior to heading off to war on the USS West Virginia. Mother perked up and was excited to recall the early days. Vernon and Marcella Sparks were married in Bell, California in March of 1940. Dad was home when they were first married. Mother talked fondly and with excitement about their time together in Long Beach, California. She mentioned that they frequently went out dancing with friends and for dinner. Mother said while raising her voice, "Dad drank too much," suggesting that alcohol was very much part of his life at the time, and so it was for Navy men in general. I believe Mother went right along with all the partying at the time as well. They drove around and explored Southern California and the beaches. "The Long Beach Pike" was a favorite hang-out for Navy men and their spouses before the war. The Pike was an early Long Beach amusement park, close to the marina area, catering to military men and women during and after WWII. I can remember going to The Pike with my brother Danny when we were kids. Later it became an unhealthy area and was completely renovated into a modern beach town tourist area attracting people of all social standing.

Mother described Dad as a very confident, egotistical, and somewhat aggressive man with a high level of testosterone. But he was not abnormally angry, nervous, anxious, or upset. He seemed to sleep well with no apparent mood changes. Mother describes the time before the war as the happiest time in her life with her new husband. Mother became pregnant with Jerry around December 1940 or January 1941 shortly before Dad steamed off to Hawaii on the USS West Virginia. Jerry was born in September 1941, 3 months before the Japanese attack on Pearl Harbor on December 7, 1941. Dad did not meet his first born son, Jerry, until he was around 16 months old. This visit back home was very brief. Dad was assigned to Shore Patrol in Pearl Harbor right after the Japanese bombing of Pearl Harbor for well over a year until he was reassigned to the newly commissioned USS Belle Grove in August 1943. Dad did not come home at all until just before WWII ended in August 1945. According to Mother, Dad came home a complete mess and was "locked up" in the US Naval Hospital in Shoemaker, California for an extended period. Dad's battle fatigue condition got the best of him and he was considered too unstable to not have supervision and close treatment before being released to function as a normal individual and responsible Navy man. All of this history is described in Vernon H. Sparks' official medical records approved by the Naval Board of Medical Survey from this time and is detailed to the extent that it appears his condition was very serious. Mother was not even allowed to visit with him with son Jerry for quite awhile until he was considered stable. Mother mentioned she was very disappointed since Dad was gone so long, and he didn't even get a chance to celebrate the end of WWII right away with everyone else, including being absent again as a father of first born son Jerry, around 4 years old. Following is quoted from the medical records right after Dad returned from the Asiatic Pacific Theater serving on the USS Belle Grove.

This man was admitted to the sick list on July 23,1945 at the USNT&DC, Shoemaker, California, with combat fatigue, complaining of nervousness and irritability, and he was transferred here the same date. According to the man's statement, accepted by the board, he was in good health until the onset of his present symptoms. He was aboard the USS West Virginia, torpedoed at Pearl Harbor, and was trapped below decks but worked his way clear and swam under burning oil to get away from the ship. Since that time he has been moderately apprehensive while at sea and his symptoms became aggravated during the 7 Pacific invasions with "general quarters practically all the time." He returned to the mainland in June 1945, and all symptoms have subsided since admission, with psychotherapy and reassurance. The physical examination and all indicated special studies are negative for essential organic pathology. The psychiatric examination reveals a subsiding fatigue state in a previously stable individual with good insight and excellent service motivation.

From my own perspective, and considering the standard mental health medical treatment procedures of the time, I can imagine that this was a very scary place for Dad to spend 60 days or so until released in September 1945.

Following is the specific diagnosis of Vernon H. Sparks:

Combat Fatigue, #2171 Origin: Not Misconduct. Tense, nervous, anxious, has shoulder that is easily dislocated. Symptoms came on while at sea, tour of combat duty of 66 months ending some 6 weeks ago. Sleeps poorly, wakens often, nightmares of combat. Appetite is variable. He is sensitive to noise and crowds. Startle Reaction. He is moody at times. Not suicidal. He is fatigued."

Dad was released from the hospital and returned to duty on September 6, 1945. All of these symptoms are included in the modern set of symptoms referred to as Post Traumatic Stress Disorder (PTSD). Dad was severely damaged emotionally during his extended combat experience during WWII, not including additional combat sea duty during the Korean War. Dad came home a different man, who needed extensive treatment for a condition that was not well understood at the time.

References:

Battle fatigue: The World War II name for what is known today as post-traumatic stress, this is a psychological disorder that develops in some individuals who have had major traumatic experiences (and, for example, have been in a serious accident or through a war). The person is typically numb at first but later has symptoms including depression, excessive irritability, guilt (for having survived while others died), recurrent nightmares, flashbacks to the traumatic scene, and overreaction to sudden noises. Post-traumatic stress became known as such in the 70s due to the adjustment problems of some Vietnam veterans. http://www.medterms.com/script/main/art.asp?articlekey=2443

Posttraumatic Stress Disorder (PTSD) Causes:
http://www.medicinenet.com/posttraumatic_stress_disorder/article.htm

Virtually any trauma, defined as an event that is life-threatening or that severely compromises the emotional well-being of an individual or causes intense fear, may cause PTSD. Such events often include either experiencing or witnessing a severe accident or physical injury, receiving a life-threatening medical diagnosis, being the victim of kidnapping or torture, exposure to war combat or to a natural disaster, exposure to other disaster (for example, plane crash) or terrorist attack, being the victim of rape, mugging, robbery, or assault, enduring physical, sexual, emotional, or other forms of abuse, as well as involvement in civil conflict. Although the diagnosis of PTSD currently requires that the sufferer has a history of experiencing a traumatic event as defined here, people may develop PTSD in reaction to events that may not qualify as traumatic but can be devastating life events like divorce or unemployment.

Putting out the fires on the USS West Virginia at Pearl Harbor (U.S. Navy)

My father Vernon's behavior, from the beginning, had always created confusion and many questions were never answered. While he was scary and abusive with an authoritarian style, he did teach me a few things that continue guiding me to this day. For one, I have a great respect for the US Navy and the military as a whole. The strong "command" type leadership is critical in time of war. He also taught me how to survive on my own. He made me want to succeed enough to "show him" how successful his son could be. Absolutely nothing could get in my way. I had no desire to live in a highly dysfunctional life style the rest of my life. There was no better motivation to succeed! I knew I could do better than this...

I owe my success in part to my Dad, but not without a high price. I call this "collateral damage" from living in a family culture affected by Post Traumatic Stress Disorder (PTSD). At that time, men at war and coming home from war were too proud to share their stories and admit that anything in the way of mental illness was on the table for discussion. My Dad was no different than thousands of veterans with similar symptoms, especially those who were battle weary and emotionally damaged. The children and wives and others close to these men would have to experiment and learn how to navigate our way through a terrible circumstance. We did it well, but not without scars that often show. WWII has been in our past for well over a half century, and most of the "Greatest Generation" passed on, but the effects of PTSD carry forward just like bad genes. We are still feeling the effects of WWII when PTSD was not studied and treatment was minimal. As a result, we are just beginning to address the realities of PTSD, including diagnosis and treatment, along with complete recovery from this unfortunate mental illness is now possible. **"Men, especially those serving in the military, were not expected to display emotions of any kind."** This is an often heard but very significant general statement of that time that suggests one of the major reasons combat veterans rarely shared their experiences and less than healthy emotional feelings. As a kid I always wondered why Dad never hugged or kissed me. He started hugging and kissing, including expressing healthy emotions later in life, however.

I probably could have been more understanding had I known about Dad's diagnosis of "battle fatigue" now referred to as PTSD. It was a terrible problem, and still is today. I also recognize that a mental disorder of this type is not likely clear in the minds of victims of abuse, especially young children. The men at sea fighting in WWII had only alcohol on liberty and a structured life style on the ship; both serving as a non-clinical and less than effective treatment plan. Not to excuse Dad's abusive behavior at times, however, the more one understands about mental disorders the easier it is to avoid hate. Hate, from my experience, is a killer of a healthy mental disposition and peace of mind. Dad needed help but at that time it wasn't very macho to whine or to seek out support. Those sailors who survived the war felt guilty for living, a typical human reaction among survivors of traumatic events where close friends or loved ones are killed. The only things that held them together after all that time at war were thinking of their families and the buddies they fought with. It was really hard for them emotionally when a close buddy was killed. Otherwise, they held together pretty good while at war using a "dead already" mindset, kind of like the "dead man walking" idea. Once they got home all hell broke loose in very visible and uncontrolled ways. Families did not understand, nor did they feel comfortable spilling the beans about their illness that might keep them from working. It was a vicious circle at that time and very sad to say the least. Our heroes from WWII had to live with PTSD or "battle fatigue" without adequate diagnosis and treatment. PTSD is consequently an invisible war wound that does not heal nor go away easily.

USS Belle Grove Asiatic Pacific Theater War Cruise

Dad spent the remaining months of WWII aboard the USS Belle Grove (LSD-2). The Belle Grove was commissioned on August 9, 1943. The crew photograph included in this story was taken right after the USS Belle Grove was commissioned. Vernon H. Sparks, BMC is the third Chief Petty Officer (CPO) from the left in the second row designated for all CPO's. Dad is sitting right behind the Commanding Officer. His hat is cocked a bit to his left.

After reading stories about the Pacific War and looking for information on websites, I found the USS Belle Grove website for all crew members starting with those who are still alive from WWII to those who served in the Korean War and Vietnam. I could find only two crew members still alive from my father's war cruise shown on the "USS Belle Grove War Cruise Map." Both men joined the Navy in 1943 after the Belle Grove was commissioned and just before it steamed to the Pacific Asiatic Theater to fight in 7 campaigns noted on the map. Both of these men joined the Navy at 17. Charlie Minter actually knew my dad and has been in touch with me, including providing an e-mail of how he remembered dad as "bos'n

Sparks" at the time. Cliff Viereck was on the engineering team and did not know Vernon, but provides an account of life on the Belle Grove during the war cruise, including the Iwo Jima battle, which I will use as a resource in writing the story about this famous ship that served in seven campaigns and was one of the most decorated in the Asiatic Pacific Theater. The men serving on the Belle Grove did not receive liberty until 25 months of battle at sea. The first liberty was in Singapore as noted on the War Cruise Map.

When dad completed his shore patrol assignment in Hawaii in the summer of 1943, it had been almost two years since the Japanese attack on Pearl Harbor. He was able to return home briefly for a few weeks before returning to war in the Pacific. He was promoted to BMC in 1943 and subsequently assigned to the USS Belle Grove (LSD-2). He was on the commissioning crew on August 9, 1943. Dad was one of three Pearl Harbor survivors on the BG. He was held in high esteem along with all who survived this Japanese surprise attack on our Pacific Naval Fleet on December 7, 1941. The BG would become one of the most decorated war ships in the Pacific Asiatic Theater serving in 7 campaigns, included the now famous Iwo Jima battle. LSD means Landing Ship Dock. These mighty ships were cleverly designed as a sea going ship repair station deployed in the campaigns to repair damaged ships at sea, and to land marines on the beach, and to recover the wounded and killed.

These men, heroes to be sure, who landed on the beaches of places like Iwo Jima, knew they were given a 50% or less chance of survival. My dad carried marines onto shore and risked his life as well, but never felt he was a hero or was doing what his fellow marines had to do. In other words, he wasn't exactly on a suicide mission like the rest, so he as well as most sailors felt guilty most of the time for being alive. This kind of guilt lives with men following the war for the rest of their lives. It is one of the symptoms creating the conditions for PTSD. Interesting but tragically, the feeling of guilt also lives with the abused spouses and children of surviving combat veterans. Guilt is evident in most cases of PTSD whether from combat, surviving an accident where others were killed, or from living in a toxic family culture as a survivor of long term abuse.

This subject requires much more research to determine why the conditions of abuse cause guilt similar to the guilt experienced by survivors of war and other tragedies that cause trauma to minds and body. There must be a connection in the mix that relates back to the

"I'm not deserving or good enough" mindset. This kind of feeling happens to me all the time, much more so as a younger man. And this kind of guilt feeling can be destructive and cause a person not to manage success very well. We deserve failure but not success so to speak. Consequently, self-destructive behavior can emerge if one is not able to cope with the reality and benefits of success. But we who suffer with PTSD work hard to be successful and to prove our worthiness. Once achieving success, especially when it appears to be surreal, a PTSD survivor can be overcome with guilt feelings and the need to be punished, even if it is self inflicted.

I will never forget how I felt when being honored with the highest recognition for excellence at Nortel Networks in 1989, "Masters." I was walking to the stage to accept congratulations from our CEO, and to receive my coveted Baume & Mercier watch. I felt less than deserving! I was in the prime of my career and had just been promoted to vice president sales, independent carriers i.e., General Telephone, United Telephone, CenturyTel, et al., of our fiber optics transmission group, and was one of the highest paid employees in the company. I earned my success with very hard work and highly recognized leadership. How could I not feel deserving? Most who suffer the symptoms of PTSD will note they often feel less than deserving. My research will reveal more about the implications of PTSD symptoms and how it affected me and other family members over the years.

Duty aboard the USS Belle Grove during WWII

The following is an account of the Belle Grove's participation in the Invasion of Iwo Jima during February 1945, as remembered by Clifford E. Viereck, MM2. Cliff was aboard the Belle Grove from 15 Aug 1944 to 28 Mar 1946. He now resides in Sunnyside, Washington, and can be reached by e-mail at cliffv@embarqmail.com. He would like to hear from any of his former shipmates.

July 23, 2000 (as edited by Steve Sparks)

Cliff E. Viereck enlisted in the Navy at the age of 17 in 1943. Following boot camp training in Farragut, Idaho, he was sent to engineering school at the Ford Motor Company in Dearborn, Michigan. The school was built by Henry Ford expressly to train young Navy students to operate and maintain machinery and equipment on steam and diesel ships.

Henry Ford Sr. personally welcomed new Naval students to the school. Using commercial resources at the time to prepare for fighting in WWII was an excellent example of America at its best during that period. Every part of society came together as a team to use all natural resources effectively during a critical time in history.

On March 15, 1944, after completing school at the Ford Motor Company, some of the sailors were sent to the Destroyer Base in San Diego for additional training on operating and repairing Hallscott gas and GM diesel engines used in amphibious landing craft called LCVPs and LCMs. These landing craft were built to carry men and equipment to the landing beaches in the Pacific and in Europe. LCVPs were 36 feet in length and could normally carry 36 troops. LCMs were 50 or 60 feet long and could transport troops, a small cannon or a 35-ton General Sherman tank.

Cliff volunteered for small boat duty but did not anticipate his transfer to Coronado, CA for amphibious training. He spent the next six weeks landing on the beaches in very uncomfortable surf getting sea sick, bruised and wet. During the period of May 13 through May 23, he was attached to the USS Hunter Liggett practicing amphibious landings from the ship with Marines from Camp Pendleton.

Cliff recalled the training and landings clearly. The boats used for training were early versions of the LCVPs with the helm perched precariously on the fantail of the boat. Boat crews for the VPs consisted of the Coxswain, two deckhands (seamen) and one engineer. Although some of the new trainees were not Coxswains it did not excuse them from operating the boat during landings. Due to large waves and rough seas it was hazardous to be perched on the stern of the craft and maintain footing to avoid breaking an arm from the wheel or being tossed in the ocean. These early designed boats were often gas powered and had a strange way of catching fire causing damage to men and boats during the landings.

On May 31, 1944, Cliff and his shipmates departed San Diego on the aircraft carrier Franklin for Pearl Harbor and other points in the Pacific. The Navy was noted for not knowing exactly where they should place some of its personnel. Cliff and his fellow shipmates were transported from island to island until they finally returned to Pearl Harbor on August 15, 1944. They were assigned to the USS Belle Grove, a Landing Ship Dock (LSD), lovingly referred to as a "Large Sitting Duck".

The USS Belle Grove (LSD-2) was 490 feet long. The ship carried one five inch cannon on the foredeck and many forty millimeter and smaller guns to make it look threatening. "We never seemed to do well hitting anything," recalled Cliff. He recalls once when returning from New Guinea to the Philippines sighting a free floating mine. The gunners spent some time attempting to hit and remove the hazard for other ships. Finally it was decided to continue on their way and report the sighting to other ships. The main purpose or use for LSDs was to carry amphibious craft to a landing site. The ship would ballast down filling the 390-foot well deck with water to load and unload landing craft. The Belle Grove had only two LCVPs (Landing Craft Vehicle Personnel) assigned specifically for the ships use.

With the training Cliff received, he would have normally been assigned to an amphibious boat crew, a group of men and boats that would continue to train as a unit. Rather, he was assigned to "A" division aboard the Belle Grove. The "A" division is responsible for repairs and maintenance of all auxiliary equipment aboard ship as well as manning the boats assigned specifically to the ship. The BG had only two boats, # 1 and # 2 boats that were positioned port and starboard.

The next several months the BG toured the Pacific Asiatic Theater making the D-Day landing October 20, 1944, at Leyte, and S-Day landing at Luzon (Lingayan Gulf) January 9, 1945.

IWO JIMA Experience Remembered

Cliff Viereck recalls his personal experience during the invasion of Iwo Jima. Cliff wishes to express that his participation was insignificant and in no way suggests his role was more than just being there supporting the real heroes of this campaign. The supreme sacrifices made by the 4th, 5th, and 3rd Marine divisions during the 36 days of battle far outshadow all of the support groups that took part in the invasion.

Cliff recalls that they were seldom informed or knew where they were headed next. But on February 7, 1945, they arrived at Guam. They ballasted down to receive 20 LCMs Landing Craft Mechanized with crews that were filled to the gunwales with powder and shell for the landing at Iwo Jima. The ship immediately departed Guam for Saipan a few miles away. They left Guam with their "load of firecrackers" for safety reasons.

The boat crews from the LCMs were assigned to the Belle Grove for the landing on Iwo Jima.

On February 17, they departed Saipan arriving early February 19. Cliff remembers truthfully that D Day at Iwo Jima there was no delay ballasting down and getting those ammunition loaded craft away from the BG. The purpose of those boats full of ammunition was to replace the ammunition used by the warships to shell Iwo Jima the previous few days.

On that first day the Belle Grove and the ship's crew, with the exception of the LCM boats and crews, were mere spectators to the landings and the battle taking place on the beaches. Cliff and his shipmates witnessed the continuing bombing and rockets that continually hit Mt. Surabachi and other areas near the beaches. As night approached most of the ships not needed would go out to sea and return at dawn.

D-Day plus one the Belle Grove returned to the Island. The primary duty for the ship was to function as a dry dock for the damaged boats. The ship would ballast down and receive the boats that required repair. Most of the repairs were for the propellers and propeller shafts bent from the beach landings. The second day Cliff was assigned to the ship's boat #2. Cliff was 19 at this time and somehow never rose above being the junior on the team, which assured Cliff of a position on jobs that were not desirable. Normally the ship's boats would not be involved in actual landings, but for some reason the skipper must have volunteered the two ship's boats to participate in a joint effort with other ship's boats to form a boat group that would transport Marines to the landing beaches. That seemed unusual to their boat crew because it would have been beneficial to team together prior to making such a serious venture. Never the less, being young and gung ho provided him and his shipmates with all the necessary strength to proceed as directed; besides, they had no choice.

The BG's boats were directed to a troop transport that was loaded with Marines. Eight other LCVPs also arrived at the ship and all went along side the transport to load Marines. The Marines boarded the boats using cargo nets. When the boats were all loaded someone must have felt it would be appropriate to have an officer in charge of this rag tag unit of boats. "It was our lucky day to have a young lieutenant j.g. come down the cargo net to get into our boat," Cliff recalls. One of his buddies on the ship tossed him a bullhorn that became his security blanket.

Cliff remembers his concern about the training this officer had received. Among other questions designed to prolong the lives of others, Cliff wondered, "Did he know the fundamentals about the landing procedure? Did he know which of the several beaches to land at?" As it turned out he had received some training in amphibious landing procedures and coupled with his training they agreed on several important life saving points.

There was a procedure that was generally accepted prior to hitting the beach. The ten boats in the group with approximately 36 Marines in each boat rendezvoused and headed towards the beach. The first step prior to landing is to circle up just like the settlers used to do. The lieutenant did well to accomplish that exercise using his bullhorn and arm signals. Following that, and just before heading to the beach, one employs the signal to form a line of assault. Again the lieutenant did well because they formed that line and headed for their destination on the beaches of Iwo Jima.

Each of the boat crew members has a specific job to do upon landing. The coxswain's job is probably the most important. He has to keep the boat at right angles to the beach to prevent the boat from broaching (turning sidewise and swamping or sinking right at the beach). During landing the waves were very large and the beach angle was very steep preventing a level landing. The job of the engineer is to keep the motor running primarily by keeping the sea water from becoming restricted due to the volcanic ash on the beach. There is a dual strainer that requires constant attention. The engineer and the two deck hands must disengage the ramp and lower the ramp with a hand winch. The added problem on this beach was the steep angle that did not allow the ramp to drop freely.

Due to the clutter of sunken and damaged boats and vehicles on the beach the wave of BG's ten boats could not land on the same section of beach. Cliff could not recall seeing any of the boats again with the exception of the other ship's boat #1 and that was the next day.

In Cliff's opinion, several things must occur in the minds of Marines landing and the Navy boys taking them to the beach. In Cliff's mind, he thought of two things, he was scared to death and thought about his mother who he knew worried about him. He distinctly recalls thinking that if she only knew "I was OK and standing unharmed," it would be better for her. Cliff's most profound thought when they actually hit the beach was for the young Marines delivered to the beach. They were all Cliff's age and they had transported them to a place they might never return from. This feeling was supported by the next surprising event; the beach master would not let them depart the beach after landing the Marines. The boat crews were ordered to remain in the surf and cluttered beach until they were loaded with as many wounded Marines as they could hold—all were on stretchers. They also took one Japanese soldier with a head wound.

After departing the beach, they attempted to deliver the wounded to any ship that would accept them. There was a hospital ship there but Cliff did not know why they were not able to take the wounded to that ship. The boat crew had difficulty finding a ship that would take them. Finding a ship that would take the Japanese was even more difficult. They finally threatened to throw him overboard if someone did not accept him.

The boat crew did not have radios then and no specific orders as to what to do next. They delivered the lieutenant to his ship and he was happy to be shed of them. When he was ascending the gangplank they called back to him, "You left your bullhorn behind." He yelled back, "Keep it and hope I never see you all again." Cliff could not recall all the events of the day but darkness was falling and they were drifting around off the Island. Their ship, the Belle Grove, was nowhere in sight. Most of the ships had to retreat further out to sea leaving only the control boats and some of our landing craft drifting around. It was not in the plan to remain on the small boat all night but that is what happened. He recalls it was cold and not very exciting. They tried to stay a distance away from the beach but not too far out to sea. The control boats and Marines continually shot star shells so they could visualize the enemy swimming out to our boats.

The Belle Grove returned the next day to pick up its chicks. They were very happy to be back aboard and spent the next month repairing damaged boats.

Although Cliff could not remember my Dad Vernon or did not know him, his account provided me with a most personal connection to Cliff and gave me the feeling of what my father and others typically experienced

while preparing for and in battle serving on the USS Belle Grove in the Asiatic Pacific Theater during a critical strategic war cruise during WWII. Steve Sparks...

USS Belle Grove © 2008 | all rights reserved

The above presentation of my father's naval service decorations was created by my brother Dan for our mother, Marcella, after Dad passed away in 1998. She was able to think of the very positive attributes of her husband as a young man. It really comforted her in a time of grief. It also served to remind all of us of Dad's Honorable Naval Service. We can be very proud of his service to the country and his accomplishments during his 22 year career in the U.S. Navy.

The following photo was received from an old shipmate of my Dad, Cliff Viereck. I provided Cliff's account of duty on the USS Belle Grove earlier. His son Mike keeps all his dad's archives and made a high resolution photo of the commission crew, 2nd half of photo. My father, Vernon, known as "Bosn Sparks" at the time, is the third CPO from the right in the 2nd row right behind the CO. His hat is cocked to left, that's the way he wore his hat in those days. The shot was taken in the ballast area of the ship where damaged ships would come in to be repaired and sent back out to sea.

BMC Sparks in second row from right, third Chief Petty Officer

This is an e-mail from another shipmate of Dad's, Charlie Minter, who communicated with me as a result of making an inquiry on the USS Belle Grove Association website. The account is highly emotional to me because it describes my Dad in a very personally connecting way.

Hi Charles,

I can't hold back my emotions while typing this response. My brothers, and sister, and I will hold your e-mail dear to our hearts, and can never thank you enough for sharing the information about our Dad, Vernon, who passed away in 1998. He was definitely on the rough side with us, but we all learned how to survive in a tough world. As soon as I can get myself composed, I will call you to talk more. I'm writing a story about our Dad's war years and about how "battle fatigue" affected war weary WWII veterans like you and our dad. You are all heroes from the "Greatest Generation" and we can never honor or thank you enough for your service to our country. I've studied the Asiatic Pacific Theater and know how terrible this war was. My brother Jerry served in the Navy for

30 years and retired as a Warrant Officer, and knows this history well too. I served for a very short time in the Navy as an RM3. The Navy was the start of my very successful career in the telecommunications industry. With all respect and gratitude,

Steve Sparks
Depoe Bay, Oregon

Quoting Charles Minter <crminter26@ntelos.net> :

Steve- My name is Charlie Minter. I served under Sparks on deck of the Belle Grove. I went aboard on Oct 43 and was assigned to the 3rd. division aft. The first chewing out I ever got was from Bosn Sparks. He had the longest arm of any one I ever saw. You didn't fool with him. He was fair as anyone this little 17 year old ever knew. . He could get loud too. I thought a lot of him on the ship. He was good to me as he got me a pie job on the ship, but with the understanding I would keep his uniforms pressed at all time which I did. Hope this helps. Charles R. Minter.

The following map shows the seven Asiatic Pacific Campaigns of the USS Belle Grove (LSD-2).

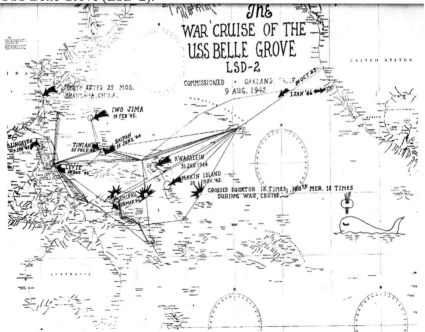

Following many months at sea and in many battles, the USS Belle Grove (LSD-2) was a war weary looking ship that needed an overhaul. USS Belle Grove earned seven battle stars for World War II service and seven campaign stars for Vietnam War service. http://www.navsource.org/archives/10/12/1202. htm. The BG was overhauled and returned to service for the Korean and Vietnam Wars.

USS Belle Grove (LSD-2) conducting sea trials August 1943 in San Francisco Bay (http://www.navsource.org/archives/10/12/1202.htm)

The following letter of recommendation to my father just before WWII ended makes me proud indeed. No one can take away the dedication and honorable service of Vernon H. Sparks, BMC, US Navy.

Now that you know quite a bit about Vernon H. Sparks and his WWII history, it is equally important to discuss the family as a whole and their experiences growing up and living with a father who had been severely affected emotionally by WWII, especially the surprise Japanese attack on Pearl Harbor on December 7, 1941. To help understand the implications of intergenerational PTSD, this author will start by looking back on my

Mother, Marcella's life, and then move on to the rest of the Sparks clan, including myself. I received significant input in writing as well as many phone interviews with my siblings and my mom, Marcella, including personal visits along the way. Putting all these lives and experiences in context will help readers to understand the dynamics of our family's behavior and the effects of intergenerational PTSD.

Dad in whites at the end of his career in the US Navy circa 1958

Marcella C. Sparks, a Wife and Mother from the Depression Era and WWII

It was quite clear from my Dad's medical records that my mother, Marcella, hated the Navy and everything it was doing to him from keeping him away for long periods to having an effect on his disposition. Mother appeared to be supportive on the surface, but took every opportunity to nag Dad morning, noon, evening, and even during the middle of the night when he was home. Her complaining and badgering never seemed to stop.

Mother was traumatized too from the war, and from being alone with Jerry for almost two years while Dad was fighting in the Pacific Asiatic Theater aboard the USS Belle Grove. She had a couple of friends, and one special friend, Julie, whose husband was gone as well, so the two of them were able to help each other during some very difficult times while waiting for the war to end and the return of their husbands safely home for good. Julie had a daughter, Melinda, who Jerry loved to hang out with too. Mother used Julie as a babysitter when she needed a little freedom and the favor was returned. The babysitting would generally take place at Julie's since she had an inside bathroom. Mother's apartment had a bathroom down the hallway, shared by all residents of the floor.

My Brother Jerry's memories show Mother as a relatively happy and loving person when they were home alone living on Scott Street in San Francisco. Waiting for Dad to come home from the war became a normal way of life for most married women at the time. They essentially learned how to be single parents and learned how to be independent. Jerry believes mother really liked being independent, raising a son, working part time for Beaman's Bags in San Francisco. She was making some extra money and having a pretty good life with a couple of good friends to hang out with and this period was considered a happy time for my brother Jerry. He and mother were very close, and she behaved as a model parent in his view. Jerry felt loved and secure at the time. He really didn't care about having a father around so to speak. He had the undivided attention of his mother. All this happiness and security changed when Dad came home. Guess you could say the party was over.

Spouses were affected first with PTSD symptoms but were essentially ignored and only wanted to be supportive of their loving husbands who were fighting for their freedoms. In my mother's case, she appeared to be on the selfish side for the most part. She barely finished the 7th grade before leaving school. I believe her goal was to find a husband, raise a family, and be a loving wife and good mother.

Marcella C. Sparks was born in St. Paul, Minnesota in September, 1918, to Albert and Nettie Schaub. Both Al and Nettie were born to parents who migrated from the old country, Luxembourg to be exact. Mother grew up during the Depression years, in a Catholic family culture with very little money. She hated her older sister Lydia who she felt got all the attention when growing up. She disliked Lydia so much that they didn't see or talk to each other for years living just blocks from each other in Tacoma, Washington during the 1960's when Dad was finally out of the Navy pursuing a career with the Federal Correctional Institution.

Growing up during the "Great Depression" years was a huge disadvantage for women during my mother's time. Most women had to quit school at an early age like my mother. They needed to get to work early on and try to find a husband to start a family as a way to survive. Women today are lucky and blessed to have the opportunity to look past a 7th grade education and hold off getting married and starting a family too early with often disastrous consequences. In the case of my mother, Marcella, she made it through the 7th grade then started working to help her family during these challenging years. Yes, she had dreams as a young woman, as most did at that time. But those dreams gave way to the realities of the times. Women were not considered productive in the broader economy and assumed to be homemakers at best, with little or no opportunities for even completing high school let alone entering college and pursuing a career in a male dominated world.

Mother met Dad not too long after he entered the US Navy in 1936. Of course, he was rarely home between the time they started courting each other and the time they were married in 1940. Mother was good friends with Dad's sister Juneth during that time, so this became the connection to my mother's chances of succeeding in finding a husband and having a family as the ideal way to survive during this time. Not too long after they were married Dad was off to sea duty again right after she became pregnant with my older brother Jerry. The Japanese attack on Pearl Harbor in December, 1941, created an impossible situation for a new marriage to thrive and grow.

My Dad was gone, really gone, and Mother was not sure he would even come back. Consequently, many women of that time ended up being single parents, without an education, alone without a husband or friends or even a job. Pile on the Depression years growing up and the trauma of WWII and you get an awful case of PTSD that starts to affect the kids before "battle fatigued" Dad arrives home from the war. Mother was a basket case by the end of WWII as were no doubt many thousands of women in the same position at that time. Newly married, small children, no husband, no money, lonely, and uneducated; a very negative combination of challenges and hardly anyone cared or even thought about it. These wives and mothers had to tough it out on their own since their war hero husbands were sacrificing their lives in Europe and in the Pacific. As a kid during the war my brother Jerry carried the most burden of living with Mother during that time. My guess is Jerry had to grow up really fast, and his story follows.

Sister Laura's special memory of a visit with Marcella

My sister Laura adds a special touch and perspective of our mother, Marcella, during a visit some years ago. Laura's relationship with Mother changed dramatically when Dad passed away in 1999. At long last a lost daughter is able to reconcile with her mother and begin building a loving friendship, but not without challenges. Laura's experience in a toxic home environment took its toll with all the markings of disappointment, tough life experiences, and the insecurity that comes with feeling your mother or father do not love you. This feeling for Laura would start to change during this visit and the 11 years since represents a major turning point in her life to heal, discover self worth, and make amends.

Sister Laura with me at one of our favorite Oregon beaches, summer 2011

Laura was happy Mother was coming down to visit for a couple of weeks following Dad's passing in 1999. Laura and her husband Terry just bought a home. Terry wasn't sick yet and they had a comfortable room for Mother to make herself at home. "The visit went very well, and was actually enjoyable," Laura exclaimed with enthusiasm. The background story here is that most visits, if not all of them, with Mother were extremely challenging over the years, and most often everyone was exhausted after a visit and couldn't wait for her to leave or for us to get out of town. As an example, Laura shares this experience, which represents the usual trigger for disharmony and another challenging visit with Mother. As Laura tells the story, Mother launched into a speech about how she taught Laura how to make potato salad, but she still couldn't make it right. Laura didn't put enough mustard in the salad according to Mother. The worst part of Mother's tutorial and the statement that could have caused "WWIII" again for the 100th time, she shouted, "that isn't the way Danny likes it; he likes my potato salad the best because I put enough mustard in my recipe!" Laura told me she felt like telling her to make it herself; however, as the ever compromising codependent, Laura added more mustard to Mother's satisfaction. Laura felt blessed with all the rare attention from her mother, so escalating the matter was not in the cards this day. Laura felt that a little negative didn't matter, as the last time she received special attention from her Mother was when Dad passed away. At that time and totally unexpected for Laura, Mother mended differences in a brave, honest and compassionate way. Mother needed her only daughter by her side at Dad's funeral and friendship became possible for the first time.

Prior to Dad passing away, Mother never seemed to be sensitive enough to look past her own needs and focus on others, especially her children. It is apparent from Laura's experience that kids must know their parents love them and care about their feelings. Mother spent most of her married life preoccupied with Dad and trying to help him heal and be a happy man, ignoring her children to a large extent. Laura felt abandoned for many years following being sent to live with her brother Danny and sister-in-law, Marcia, when she was barely 16. Laura has suffered clear symptoms of PTSD for most of her life due to the emotional and physical abuse during her young life living in this troublesome home. Once her big brothers were gone, it became even tougher for her to survive. The baggage carried forward for many years and lots of struggles, but now with Dad gone, there appeared to be an opportunity for both mother and daughter to become close friends.

Laura planned a few outings for just mother and daughter to bond. One special day happened to be Mother's birthday. She took Mother to Shore Line Village in Long Beach for a special lunch. The Lighthouse was a favorite. They serve some of the best seafood and it is right on the water.

Mother is very sentimental about Long Beach. She and Dad were married in Long Beach where they spent Dad's 6 weeks of shore leave until he shipped out to Pearl Harbor on the USS West Virginia. The following is Laura's recollection of what Mother shared with her that day while reminiscing the early days of marriage in Long Beach.

It was 1939 or 1940, in St. Paul Minn. Mother was about 19 or 20 years old, attending a girl's finishing school in St. Paul when she met Juneth Sparks who was also attending the same school. They soon became good friends, even though Juneth was 2 years younger. They found a lot of common interests and ran in the same social circles.

Europe was at war and Japan was becoming very hostile in the Pacific. Surely the US would be joining soon. It was the beginning of another World War. Young able bodied men were enlisting in the United States military, and were almost immediately shipped out to various parts of Europe and the Pacific. It was expected and thought to be most honorable to serve our country. Eligible young men of dating age were becoming scarce in St. Paul. Short courtships and quick marriages were the norm. Men and women were anxious to tie the knot and even start a family before shipping out to far off destinations that were kept secret. If the men were lucky to come home alive, they knew it could be many months and even years before they would see our shores again. They wished to have a loved one waiting and writing to them.

Since Mother was ending an unsuccessful relationship with a young man, her friend Juneth suggested that she meet her older brother, Vernon. Vernon would be coming home for a short leave from sea duty in the Navy at that time. Dad had been in the Navy since 1936 and out at sea most of the time. Juneth encouraged her friend Marcella, and was sure she would be impressed with this tall, handsome and charming sailor.

Juneth set up a meeting between her friend Marcella Schaub and her brother Vernon Sparks, which was the beginning of a new Sparks's generation before and after WWII. Following a whirlwind of dating and romance Marcella fell in love with Vernon, a tall, blond, handsome, romantic and adventurous sailor. On that short three week leave, she spent as much time as possible with her new man, Vernon. During that time she met the rest of Sparks' family as well as introducing Vernon to the Schaub clan. Mother's parents, especially her Dad, approved of this handsome, strong and capable sailor. Mother was most happy to receive her "Pa's" approval.

The day for Vernon to ship out came too soon, much too soon to a destination he could not reveal. Marcella saw him off on a train headed towards the west coast of California, a distant seaport called Long Beach. Both of them promised to write each other as much as possible.

Marcella and Vernon wrote letters to each other for 5 months. Vernon's letters were full of news about the possible war in the Pacific, uncertain where he was going, and how much he missed Mother and hoped that they would soon see each other. His letters were full of humor in sharing his numerous adventures aboard ship and his feelings of love began to emerge more with each letter. Soon, Mother and Vernon began to speak about a possible life together, promises turning to commitments to each other as it became apparent they longed to be together.

One day Mother received the letter she had been hoping for from Vernon. The letter contained a yellow gold diamond engagement ring and a one way train ticket from St. Paul to Los Angeles, California. Vernon explained he needed an answer as soon as possible because he would be shipping out soon. The US Navy Fleet was destined for Pearl Harbor, Honolulu, Hawaii. Vernon expressed his love to Marcella and his hope of starting a family with her before he shipped out. For most military men, losing their life was ever present causing a natural tendency to start a family before heading off to combat. He promised housing for Mother in Bell, California, with some friends of his after he shipped out. This was clearly a romantic and adventurous notion for Marcella to contemplate during this time, but also scary in terms of leaving her comfort zone in St. Paul, Minnesota and being married to a man who may not come home.

The prospect of moving away was romantic and exciting to Marcella and fearful as well. She had never seen the Atlantic Coast let alone the far away Pacific Coast. Mother had never in her life been outside of Minnesota. Long Beach was very close to Hollywood and she dreamed of seeing some of her favorite exotic movie stars. Her favorite pass time for Saturdays was viewing the latest movie releases at the local theatre. Mother was somewhat anxious about being married by a Judge in California. Marcella came from a very strict Catholic family, and so she hoped the marriage would be blessed by the Catholic Church sometime in the future. Vernon, being Lutheran, agreed that he would practice the Catholic beliefs with her and the children they hoped to have.

With the blessings of her family and much anticipation Marcella boarded the train. Vernon promised to be at the Los Angeles train station in a few days to meet her when she arrived.

Mother's trip across the country was full of sites, landscapes and interesting things she had only read about in books, newspapers, and magazines or heard about on the radio. After some research I was able to conclude that Mother must have traveled on the Union Pacific from Minnesota. The passenger train traveled along the Mississippi River and then headed west across the country close to the old highway "Route 66" to the Pacific Coast, arriving in downtown Los Angeles.

When the train arrived at last to the Pacific Coast the beauty was breathtaking, just as Vernon had promised. The exotic palm trees, blue clear sky and the warm weather were wonderful. Just as Vernon promised, he was waiting at the train station with open arms. He brought along some friends with a vehicle from Bell. They were married on March 18, 1940 in Bell, California, by the justice of peace, with a promise from Vernon that they would someday be married by a Catholic priest.

They spent a blissful honeymoon in Long Beach, which was most fun and exciting to Mother. The beaches were beautiful where they spent a lot of time sunbathing while getting to know each other in the pleasant and romantic salty sea breeze. Long Beach was a fun city during those years. The city was like a huge carnival. Long Beach was a major port for the US Navy. There was an abundance of entertainment catering to sailors on shore leave. Vernon romanced mother with her first shrimp cocktail, and exotic tropical fruit drinks with tiny umbrellas. Marcella was amazed at all the fresh produce sold at outdoor farmers markets. She enjoyed avocados for the first time, oranges, lemons, grapefruit, and many other treats. She would have never known there were so many different kinds of lettuce. Fresh salads became a lifetime habit for Mother.

Long Beach had many street markets where Japanese Americans would bring produce and other goods to sell from their farms that prospered on Terminal Island. Mother told me with much sadness and regret, she had a close friendship with a young Japanese American woman, one of those vendors. The day after the Japanese attack on Pearl Harbor, Mother went in search of her friend for comfort. Everything was gone. Mother's friend and the other Japanese American vender's had just disappeared as if they were never there. This was a very sad time for Japanese Americans who became victims of WWII. Most were sent off to camps for the duration of the war.

Finally it was time for Vernon to ship out on a short training cruise to make sure the USS West Virginia was ready for the rigors of sea duty and possible combat. Marcella stayed with Vernon's friends in Bell temporarily. When Vernon took his last leave, he moved mother into an apartment on Lime Street in Long Beach. She became lifelong friends with an older couple living in the same apartments. The older couple was childless at the time, and treated Mother as a daughter. Many of Vernon's shipmate's wives were settled in the same area of Long Beach, which provided her with a good support group and new friends.

On September 11, 1941, at the old Saint Mary's by the Sea Hospital, Marcella gave birth to Gerald Vernon Sparks the first son of Vernon. On December 7, 1941, the Japanese attacked the US Navy Pacific Fleet in Pearl Harbor by complete surprise. War was declared on Japan by the President of the United States within days of this terrible historical event that changed America forever."

From my own experience and opinion, Mother seemed never to be a happy person nor had very much compassion or passion for anything except that which affected her directly in some immediate way. This kind of attitude and behavior could have resulted from the way she learned to cope during the Depression years and WWII, living with constant trauma and anxiety. She did not pursue an education and therefore was ignorant on most matters. She worked a little early in their marriage, but seemed to not be interested in anything other than homemaking. I can't even remember hobbies that could develop her creative side. She seemed to love us but didn't come to our rescue at all when Dad was acting out and on a rampage with mental and physical abuse. He was emotionally abusive toward Mother but would never ever hit her. He beat us mostly and constantly degraded our intelligence and value to the world outside. He could beat us most of the time and get away with it but could not get away with beating Mother. My mother joined Dad in beating up my brothers and me, and would complain to Dad about our behavior when he came home from sea duty or work, and the second beatings would begin. We were typically punished twice, once by Mother and then again by Dad following a drawn out complaining period that was too much for him considering his unstable mental condition.

Once Dad retired completely in the mid-80s, after 40 years of Naval and Federal service, the chaotic and hectic life style started to settle down a bit for both. The kids were all gone and relatively successful. Dad made pretty good money with a combined Navy and Federal pension. They were both comfortable and could do most things and enjoy life a bit. They both seemed to get along well. I know for sure that Mother cared deeply for Dad and can now see there was unconditional love between them and a close friendship. I say this now because it was later when the concept of unconditional love became clear to me. I really didn't know love until Judy came into my life in the early 80's. There will be more on this subject later in the story. Dad mellowed significantly when he was totally off alcohol later in life and on proper medications to keep him calm. Modern treatment of anxiety or depression, including PTSD, is in my view a miracle when you consider the alternatives. A loving spouse and understanding family is the best treatment of all for anyone suffering from the symptoms of PTSD.

Mother and Dad had the closest relationship with youngest brother Scott and his first wife, who lived in Yakima, Washington. They were not close with the rest of us to the same extent nor did they develop relationships with grandchildren. I do know they loved their grandkids and extended family, but not sure they had the energy or communication skills to develop these relationships in a healthy way. Brother Jerry lived close to them in Tacoma, Washington. Jerry had a big challenge in maintaining a positive and healthy relationship with them due to his own anger regarding the past and the abuse he suffered at the hands of his father. But Jerry was committed to helping them as they aged in every way he could. My parents paid the price, however, with Jerry's continued need to reconcile his past. Mother and Dad hated to bring up old wounds and wanted to move forward. Jerry probably needed someone else to discuss his issues and achieve the peace he was seeking. Mother and Dad were not very good listeners for this kind of dialogue and would become extremely defensive. As a result, Jerry's relationship with his parents continued to become distant and mostly conflicted.

The rest of us lived at a distance. I was in Leavenworth, Washington, Dan's home was Reno, and Laura lived in Long Beach, Ca. Consequently, we were mostly out of the line of fire and avoided conflict. Most visits were okay and we tried to avoid the demons of the past as much as possible, but it was not perfect to be sure. I will say visits were not easy. I often experienced high anxiety while visiting with my parents, especially when siblings were present. The pressures were too much and it was often an exhausting, painful experience to visit. I really believe that we were never honest enough with each other, and should have allowed the feelings to manifest during visits. But it gets back to pain. How much pain can family members handle without an extremely high price and damage to current relationships with spouses and your own extended family? This is a subject that requires a professional to sort out and address, and is way above my pay grade. How do you treat an entire family of crazy people with deep seeded problems and issues? I don't know, but feel sad about it and it goes unresolved in my life at this point.

As of the writing of this story, Marcella is still with us at 92 in Reno, Nevada. My brother Dan is her caregiver, and has been for many years now. She has dementia and fortunately lives in a dream world of love affairs and romance. She is well cared for with the benefits received from Dad's Naval and Federal service of 40 years. My brother and I, and sister, Laura have forgiven her for many abuses and lack of caring over the years, and believe it is our duty to care for her in the best way we can with respect for our Dad and the years she suffered and sacrificed during the war. I had what I thought was my last intelligent conversation with Mother during the summer of 2010, after which she suffered a stroke that affected her ability to talk and to remember the same way. She subsequently came around and became stable again by the following summer of 2011. I try to make her laugh as much as possible when on the phone. I like to go along with her love affairs and try to get her to talk about the fling she is having with these various new men in her life. She tells me, "it's none of my business," but it is fun to make her laugh. I believe she will leave us happy and in peace at some point. But the old lady is tough as nails, and mean as hell, so she could be around awhile. My hope is to see her again and continue our fun phone talks. I pray for my Mother's peace during her last years. She endured so much pain in her life.

Whether it is fair or not, as an adult, my Mother did not leave a favorable impression or role model for me. The reader has already picked this up, so I'll just be honest about it. I do love her as my Mother, and try to do the best a son can do to provide love and support at the end of her life. I have always envied those children who have great respect and admiration for their mothers. This is clearly and sadly not the case for me. On the upside, my mother did provide me with high expectations of women in general. I did not

Photo taken during my visit with Mother in June 2011

go down the road of hating women just because my mother did not meet my expectations. Rather, I've spent my life building up women in my career and promoting independence for spouses in marriage. I believe women in general have significant potential in leadership and have shown it at home, in school, and in their work for generations. I believe my mother was in the minority as far as women are represented. I have many experiences in life, including my career, where women represent the best in leadership, work ethic, mentoring, and in friendship.

My research on spouses of our war heroes shows that they paid their dues dearly and should be honored and respected for sticking by their men at war for long periods of time, not knowing of their whereabouts or whether they were alive, injured, or dead. It always took awhile during the war to get communications or to find out what was going on in the fighting theater. I'm a strong believer in forgiveness and do not believe that holding on to hateful feelings for one's entire life is a healthy posture. I want to leave this planet at peace with myself and my family, and my past. You can't do this with hate in your heart. A peaceful and loving feeling is the only way to feel close to nature and God. And God bless all the spouses who sacrificed during all wars past or present.

In the context of contemporary life, "homemaking" in the traditional way, although highly honorable, is not a generally realistic choice for the long term for either partner in a relationship where children's needs must be met every step of the way. The total emotional, nurturing, and financial needs of a family are difficult to achieve if one's spouse is not fully engaged in a professional or vocational career. It is realistic, however, to plan for mom or dad to stay home for a couple of years to provide the close care and bonding needed for a new child. This goal is only possible if both parents achieve an adequate education beyond K-12, from either an academic or a vocational institution. Our country just can't afford to support a one income family anymore. This reality started to kick-in during the 1950's and was especially apparent as boomers became adults. A huge "war chest" is necessary to minimize family debt and to provide for the education of each child. Even with this, college bound kids still need to be resourceful by getting their own loans and working along the way.

With the good education and success of both parents, dreams of family security, happiness, and a strong partnership in marriage are realistic to achieve. Still, the challenges of raising a family in a chaotic and media driven 21st century world are many. Technology affords us all a more efficient path forward, but requires education and funding as well. The demands of work and school put big pressures on families, especially those who join the military and are sent off to war. It is even more essential to plan smart as a young woman or man to avoid early pregnancies and premature responsibilities in raising a family. It is hard, very hard to get this done, and the risk of failure increases if partners do not practice a little discipline in making education a priority at the outset. I discuss this with my kids and others whenever given the opportunity. Be patient, be safe, and get educated or pay the price later, and a higher price at that. Think about your choices and how they affect others in your life before making a move. Life happens and the challenges are enormous. Don't make it harder than it needs to be. Be smart and enjoy the journey while minimizing risk. It's not an easy journey, but doing the right things right makes a huge difference. Avoid mistakes!

The following piece is included as a quote to honor my Brother Gerald V. Sparks, USN (ret.), for his courage as a child of a WWII Veteran who suffered with the symptoms of "Battle Fatigue" or Post Traumatic Stress Disorder (PTSD):

The following passage, attributed to Rear Admiral Mike McCaffrey, USN (ret.), is the best description of my Dad, Vernon H Sparks, BMC, that really got my attention. Dad behaved exactly in this manner in executing his official duties at home. But as the story goes Dad did not model good and loving behavior as a parent most of the time. I believe my brother Jerry suffered the most during his childhood and as an adult carrying the baggage of being the first son born when WWII started.

"Never forget this, a Chief can become an Officer, but an Officer can never become a Chief. Chiefs have their standards!"

Recollections of a White Hat[1]

"One thing we weren't aware of at the time, but became evident as life wore on, was that we learned true leadership from the finest examples any lad was ever given, Chief Petty Officers. They were crusty old bastards who had done it all and had been forged into men who had been time tested over more years than a lot of us had time on the planet. The ones I remember wore hydraulic oil stained hats with scratched and dinged-up insignia, faded shirts, some with a Bull Durham tag dangling out of their right-hand pocket or a pipe and tobacco reloads in a worn leather pouch in their hip pockets, and a Zippo that had been everywhere. Some of them came with tattoos on their forearms that would force them to keep their cuffs buttoned at a Methodist picnic.

Most of them were as tough as a boarding house steak. A quality required to survive the life they lived. They were, and always will be, a breed apart from all other residents of Mother Earth. They took eighteen year old idiots and hammered the stupid bastards into sailors.

You knew instinctively it had to be hell on earth to have been born a Chief's kid. God should have given all sons born to Chiefs a return option.

---

1 From *The Real Story of the USS Johnston (DD-821)*, p. 367, George A. Sites, ed.

A Chief didn't have to command respect. He got it because there was nothing else you could give them. They were God's designated hitters on earth.

We had Chiefs with fully loaded Submarine Combat Patrol Pins, and combat air crew wings in my day...hard-core bastards who remembered lost mates, and still cursed the cause of their loss...and they were expert at choosing descriptive adjectives and nouns, none of which their mothers would have endorsed.

At the rare times you saw the Chief topside in dress canvas, you saw rows of hard-earned, worn and faded ribbons over his pocket. "Hey Chief, what's that one and that one?" "Oh hell kid, I can't remember. There was a war on. They gave them to us to keep track of the campaigns." "We didn't get a lot of news out where we were. To be honest, we just took their word for it. Hell son, you couldn't pronounce most of the names of the places we went. They're all depth charge survival gee dunks." "Listen kid, ribbons don't make you a Sailor." We knew who the heroes were, and in the final analysis that's all that matters.

Many nights, we sat in the after mess deck wrapping ourselves around cups of coffee and listening to their stories. They were light-hearted stories about warm beer shared with their running mates in corrugated metal sheds at resupply depots where the only furniture was a few packing crates and a couple of Coleman lamps. Standing in line at a Honolulu cathouse or spending three hours soaking in a tub in Freemantle, smoking cigars, and getting loaded. It was our history. And we dreamed of being just like them because they were our heroes. When they accepted you as their shipmate, it was the highest honor you would ever receive in your life. At least it was clearly that for me. They were not men given to the prerogatives of their position.

You would find them with their sleeves rolled up, shoulder-to-shoulder with you in a stores loading party. "Hey Chief, no need for you to be out here tossin' crates in the rain, we can

Get all this crap aboard."

"Son, the term 'All hands' means all hands."

"Yeah Chief, but you're no damn kid anymore, you old coot."

"Horsefly, when I'm eighty-five parked in the stove up old bastards' home, I'll still be able to kick your worthless butt from here to fifty feet past the screw guards along with six of your closest friends." And he probably wasn't bullshitting.

They trained us. Not only us, but hundreds more just like us. If it wasn't for Chief Petty Officers, there wouldn't be any U.S. Navy. There wasn't any fairy godmother living in a hollow tree in the enchanted forest who could wave her magic wand and create a Chief Petty Officer.

They were born as hot-sacking seamen, and matured like good whiskey in steel hulls over many years. Nothing a nineteen year-old jay-bird could cook up was original to these old saltwater owls. They had seen E-3 jerks come and go for so many years; they could read you like a book. "Son, I know what you are thinking. Just one word of advice, DON'T. It won't be worth it."

"Aye, Chief."

Chiefs aren't the kind of guys you thank. Monkeys at the zoo don't spend a lot of time thanking the guy who makes them do tricks for peanuts.

Appreciation of what they did, and who they were, comes with long distance retrospect. No young lad takes time to recognize the worth of his leadership. That comes later when you have experienced poor leadership or let's say, when you have the maturity to recognize what leaders should be, you find that Chiefs are the standard by which you measure all others.

They had no Academy rings to get scratched up. They butchered the King's English. They had become educated at the other end of an anchor chain from Copenhagen to Singapore. They had given their entire lives to the U.S. Navy. In the progression of the nobility of employment, Chief Petty Officer heads the list. So, when we ultimately get our final duty station assignments and we get to wherever the big Chief of Naval Operations in the sky assigns us, if we are lucky, Marines will be guarding the streets, and there will be an old Chief in an oil-stained hat and a cigar stub clenched in his teeth standing at the brow to assign us our bunks and tell us where to stow our gear... and we will all be young again, and the damn coffee will float a rock.

Life fixes it so that by the time a stupid kid grows old enough and smart enough to recognize who he should have thanked along the way, he no longer can. If I could, I would thank my old Chiefs. If you only knew what you succeeded in pounding in this thick skull, you would be amazed. So, thanks you old casehardened unsalvageable son-of-a-bitches. Save me a rack in the berthing compartment."

Life isn't about waiting for the storm to pass. It's about learning to dance in the rain."

My Brother, Gerald V. Sparks

My oldest sibling suffered the most of all of us. Dad was not home from the war when he was born in September, 1941. I believe Dad was steaming toward Pearl Harbor, Hawaii, on the USS West Virginia at that time and was not able to get leave to see his first son born. When the Japanese attack on Pearl Harbor happened on December 7, 1941, Mother was scared and worried that her son would never see his Dad. She didn't know for some time whether Dad survived or not. I can imagine what she was going through at the time. She experienced constant worry and distress, trying to keep her head up, and take care of her son during a very scary time in American history. Dad was in the middle of it, the beginning of WWII.

Thousands of babies during WWII became toddlers while their fathers were away fighting for our country. Although often too young to understand completely, kids do feel and they are a lot smarter than parents think. I believe my older sibling was exceptionally intelligent and high-strung as well. Mother and son probably developed a co-dependency that served them well while Dad was away. Dad came home briefly one time during the war when his son was almost two years old. This represents a significant period of time for a child not to know his father. In my own view, there would be little or no memory of this first visit for a small toddler.

When Dad finally came home to stay after a two year absence, following his USS Belle Grove War Cruise in the Asiatic Pacific Theater, his son could have been scared and suspicious of this big man who he knew only from pictures and talk about things he didn't really understand. He was also jealous, as any child would, that this strange man was taking time away from the attention he was getting from his Mother; undivided attention. Alcohol was a big part of life at that time as well, but not a healthy component in a family damaged by war and separation. I believe my older sibling never felt comfortable or close to his dad since there was not an opportunity to bond until age 4 or 5. It is my opinion that a child experiencing a long separation could have a difficult time developing a healthy lifetime relationship with a father they did not bond with early in life. Each experience like this is not always the same, but in my own family and from my research, it is clear that long separations are difficult to overcome, especially if a parent is suffering from symptoms of PTSD or "battle fatigue" as it was called during WWII.

The following is my Brother Jerry's own account of things from his perspective. It really helps to hear directly from those who experienced the events unfolding at a very young age and attempt to come to some conclusions and helpful lessons for others to benefit under similar circumstances.

My brother's memory faded concerning the ships that Dad served on during WWII except for the USS West Virginia (BB-48). Dad's Naval records provide a very accurate record of the ships he served on and when. His first ship was the USS Tennessee (BB-43) in 1936, including a newspaper account from the St. Paul Gazette following completion of boot camp. Prior to WWII he also served on the destroyer tender USS Black Hawk (AD-9) and the gun boat, USS Sacramento (PG-19). There was the USS Long Beach (PF-34) somewhere in the mix as well. The USS Belle Grove (LSD-2) took Dad into battle in the Asiatic Pacific Theater for 25 months beginning in August, 1943. The two sister amphibious troop transport ships during the Korean War were the USS Skagit (AKA-105) and the USS Andromeda (AKA-15).

Jerry was not a fan of any of Dad's sea and war stories other than Pearl Harbor. As the years passed his stories became more embellished and fabricated, according to my brother. The details were seldom the same. Another point of interest is that Dad had campaign ribbons and medals to show where his ships were involved and unit commendations, but curiously no personal commendations (Dad's Naval records include a commendation Jerry was not aware of) except for good conduct ribbons. Jerry believed he should have been awarded the Purple Heart for Pearl Harbor. After that time, awards and medals were more organized. As a family, we plan to apply for Purple Heart on his behalf. The Pentagon now considers "battle fatigue" or PTSD an "invisible" wound of war. It is clearly a wound that cannot be seen but has huge consequences for a returning veteran with PTSD symptoms and the families affected for generations to come. PTSD is considered a legacy of war that often never heals.

Jerry was convinced that the Korean stories were untrue except for location. Each time our father returned from the two Korean cruises, he gained a ton of weight. He was senior chief on the ship and as chiefs go, he spent a lot of time in the chief's mess eating and ashore drinking. We lived in East San Diego during the first cruise on the Skagit. He sent very little money home and Mother had little more than her allotment check and had to go to the Navy Relief for help. We met the ship when she returned to Coronado. None of us recognized him at the rail when the ship tied up. Finally, Mother recognized him and he could remember her saying "He is so fat." There was an interlude at Camp Elliott when we lived in the Quonset hut. We lived in Linda Vista for the Andromeda deployment to West Pac. and Korea. Keep in mind that these troop transports did not remain away from the states as long as combat ships of the time. The last return home at Linda Vista is one to remember. Mother had no transportation to meet the ship from that far out and her kids were older and in school. Jerry thought I was old enough to remember that our dear old dad did not come home for two days after the ship tied up. When he finally showed up in a taxi, he had a new grey suit and hat to match cocked on the side of his head. Of course, the ship was his second home so he didn't need his uniforms.

Regarding the combat claims for that cruise, Dad could never swim well because of his bad shoulder and heavy smoking. The Senior Chief Boatswains Mate was always needed aboard during operations. Jerry believes it is anybody's guess where all the eulogy stories came from. Jerry feels happy that the grandchildren have favorable memories of Dad and that they have something better to believe than he did.

Regarding the war years, Jerry's memory, in bits and pieces, goes all the way back to late 1943-44. My brother agrees in saying that the post war years were scary. To survive, Jerry became a very independent kid and has more horror stories than he can count. Jerry questions, why would any parent ever leave home for hours and expect a 7 year old to baby sit for his two little brothers? Jerry recalls his sister Laura's pose when she smokes. It is the same as Mother's pose when we were little kids, and not a good example set by Mother. He also believes a good mother would not allow her 7-8 year old to walk her two little toddlers to Presidio Park from Navy Housing. According to Jerry, she turned us out every day because she was totally stressed and needed to have a few cigarettes in peace. In the author's view, my Mother's stress had much to do with these early years waiting for her husband to come home from war and sea duty. It was difficult at that time to be a single mother without a father figure at home.

Jerry goes on to say that Dad would come home late in the evening shit-faced via the CPO club after work. Dad would drive home and put on his "combat fatigue act" (Jerry's opinion) when Mother got on his case for drinking. He can't remember when he did not have a bottle hidden. As Jerry continues to tell his story, "picture moving from San Pedro to San Diego at night in an old green Hudson Terra-plane going down dark two lane hwy101 (that was the only way) car weaving, mother clutching baby Dan in the front seat and Jerry and me in the back seat. In those days, the empty whiskey bottle and other trash went out car windows. It was a relief when he had to stop the car to take a leak at the side."

Jerry talked about living in Oak Knoll shortly after I was born, Dad made his home brew in the bath tub. It was quite awhile that Mother had to supervise us washing in the sink. One good memory was that dad had a jeep (he was in charge of the brig). We would use it to go to the outdoor movies on the base. Dan was born in federal housing near San Francisco.

Jerry and Mother must have been in San Francisco at least three years. Naval records show that Dad's war years included the beginning of the war starting with the Japanese attack on Pearl Harbor and sinking of his battleship USS West Virginia (BB-48) followed by Shore Patrol looking for Japanese subs in Pearl Harbor, and finally on to the USS Belle Grove (LSD-2), newly commissioned in August, 1943, serving in the Asiatic Pacific Theater for the rest of WWII. The record does not show which ship Dad was assigned to when he returned to San Francisco after his Pearl Harbor Shore Patrol duty. But we speculate it may have been the

USS Sacramento (PG-19). Dad had one leave when Jerry was around age two and then returned to the Pacific. Jerry was too young to remember anything significant about this visit.

The Japanese attack on Pearl Harbor happened three months after Jerry was born. Dad was finally given some leave when Jerry was almost two years old. The Naval records show he came home still as a 1st class in the fall of 1942 or early 1943. His shipmate, Chuck Bull, had previous leave and visited our family on behalf of Dad well ahead of Dad's leave. From photos of that visit, I would guess Jerry's age at about 18 months. As the story goes from Mother, little Jerry thought Chuck was his Daddy! Mother always showed pictures of Dad in uniform. "Would you believe that his shipmate was a better looking sailor than our Dad?" said Jerry. Bull also had a 1st class crow according to Jerry.

When Dad finally returned home to San Francisco he was promoted to Chief Petty Officer prior to going out to sea again. His temporary duty station appeared to be out-patient status at the Naval Hospital located on Treasure Island. He was assigned to the newly commissioned USS Belle Grove (LSD-2) in August, 1943, just before she was deployed to the Asiatic Pacific Theater in support of 7 campaigns, including Iwo Jima. A photo of the USS Belle Grove commissioning crew is included and Vernon H. Sparks BMC is in the second row third Chief Petty Officer from the left. Jerry was too young to have vivid memories of the short time Dad was home before returning to the Pacific War.

The following statement reminded me of what my brother said about the photo of us right after I was born in the summer of 1946. Jerry mentioned that he felt scared of Dad at the time. My research suggests strongly that we are "collateral damage" and the legacy of WWII lives on. The research and information on PTSD and how it affects families is just beginning to surface. The following statements, quotes, and website references could well be a thread among children of a parent suffering from the symptoms of PTSD.

Mom, Dad, Jerry, and me not long after I was born in the summer of 1946

Saturday, March 3, 2007
How PTSD Affects the Veteran's Children
Children of vets with PTSD have often been ignored in discussion of the issue. Some research has been conducted - mainly on children of Vietnam vets - that is probably applicable to children of combat vets of other wars. There are a number of mechanisms used by the children: over-identification with the PTSD affected parent; secondary traumatization; a rescuer role; depression and anxiety. These children are at greater risk for behavior, academic and interpersonal problems. Jennifer Price, Ph.D. has developed a fact sheet for the National Center for PTSD that explores some of these problems. http://dutchschultz. blogspot.com/2007/03/how-ptsd-affects-veterans-children.html   A must see website addressing the affects of intergenerational PTSD in children of combat veterans.

Posted by carolsv
Labels: <u>anxiety</u>, <u>children of World War II veterans</u>, <u>secondary traumatization</u>

Anonymous said...

> You are absolutely correct!!! There is not enough said or researched about the effects of "war", but especially the "Vietnam War" on the families, and particularly the children, of Vets. As the daughter of a combat vet, I know for a fact that that war deeply affected and changed the way I was raised. There is no doubt in my mind that I (and my sister) suffer from PTSD, as a result of our childhood. While my dad deeply loved my sister and I (and never turned to drugs or alcohol), he was always an emotional rollercoaster. You never knew what may set him off. One day would be perfectly fine, and then the very next day he would explode at the smallest provocation. As a child, I learned to be fearful, cautious, and insecure about almost every move I made. This conditioning has followed both my sister and me into adulthood. Even though my sister and I have become "successful" adults (a doctor and a lawyer), we still carry the scars from the trauma of Vietnam.

Following is another quote and example of intergenerational PTSD symptoms.

> When I left my parents' home for college in 1996, at 18, I thought my problems were over, for I would no longer have to live with my father. Turns out they had just begun, for I was filled with rage, anxiety, and depression–just like him–and was so socially awkward that it was physically painful to be around other people. I did not know how to function in a normal world, for I had only ever functioned in survival mode before. When a mental health care provider told me I had symptoms of intergenerational PTSD, I didn't know what he meant. It turns out I had inherited more than my father's dark eyes and wrinkled forehead. I had his same symptoms of PTSD. —Christal Presley, United Children of Veterans

Jessie Higgins, Posted in *The World* September 1, 2011[2]:

> During a flashback, Vietnam veteran Mark Winders said, a veteran is no longer in his home with his family.

---

2 Used with permission from *Coos Bay World.*

He is in a room full of enemies who are about to kill him.

The veteran reacts to defend himself. Only when it is all over does he discover the havoc he has unleashed on his family.

Decades after the war, Winders and his friends in the Southwestern Oregon Veterans Organization's post-traumatic stress support group are working to control their PTSD.

'This stuff does not go away," said Bill Chaplin, Coos Bay. 'You just adjust. But this s--- will poison us until the day we die."

It has been years since Chaplin -- wracked with PTSD -- secluded himself in the woods. Isolation is a common reaction to PTSD, he said.

Most of the veterans in Winders' support group have been arrested at one point or another. Looking back, they think their criminal behavior was directly linked to the trauma they experienced during war.

Young soldiers returning from today's wars face some of the same symptoms. When Staff Sgt. Eddie Black returned from Iraq in 2005, understanding his feelings took years.

'I felt like a million pieces held together by Scotch tape, ready to explode at anything," he said.

Jeff Freerksen, a Coos Bay vet from the first Iraq war, pointed to a painting of a Vietnam soldier standing in a battlefield, his brow furrowed in quiet yet obvious agony.

'That look is how I feel today," Freerksen said.

ther, Jerry, always thanked Dad and a couple million others
dedicated and brave service during the two wars of his time.
portant is how one lives their lives afterwards. A good father
ully and is nurturing and loving to his children. Dad and
ver close. Dad was gone during Mother's pregnancy and
leet his father until he was almost two years old. From

Jerry's viewpoint, Dad could not handle the fact that he did not have the same bride that he dreamed about and longed to return to while in the Pacific. Jerry remembers the arguments about Mother spending too much time with me. On vacation at the Russian River, Jerry was afraid of the water because of no previous exposure. Dad forced him in the river with him and the frightening experience and the argument that ensued caused Jerry as a small boy to be non-trusting of his father. It is tough if a little boy has that kind of letdown and mistrust. According to Jerry, there were lots of parties, booze, cigarettes and dances until I was born. Mother would drink and smoke with the best of them. After that time, Jerry can't remember ever connecting with our Dad. He does remember Dad taking him fishing only once during his childhood. That was early in the morning near Vallejo when the Skagit was in the yards. Jerry caught a striped bass and loved it. Dad apparently never made an effort again to go fishing with his son. Jerry learned everything on his own and spent much time teaching his brothers Dan and me, and sister, Laura later on. Youngest brother Scott was born long after Jerry left home to join the Navy.

According to Jerry's account, our parents were in a constant struggle with finances along with Dad's drinking problem, and not being able to agree on very much was standard fair. After all, Dad was Chief and we better not disagree with his loud barking orders, never! Jerry's siblings could count on him when he was home but there was not much parenting otherwise. Mother was sick during Laura's first year. That is what gave Jerry the most experience taking care of and teaching an infant. He remembers how easy it was to potty train Laura. Jerry was left alone with Dan and me for hours at a time when we were small. He reminded me that Mother would not drive and they needed to shop, etc. Navy housing was pretty safe at that time and he could be trusted for his age. Jerry changed my diapers until I was three. Polio slowed my progress considerably. Even though Dan was younger, he was potty trained sooner than me. I became a polio victim at age 2 and suffered with muscle damage on my left side.

Finally, Jerry believed there was no excuse for Dad's abuse of him in Illinois when the family depended on him so much financially and for help with the other children.

Jerry believed that most incarcerated people lived better than he did from the army cot in the basement to the fact that he could not get enough to eat in the winter after wading through snow drifts morning and night seven days a week on his paper route. He still had to go to school. Mother did pack lunches and he was able to supplement nourishment with candy and peanuts that he bought with the change salvaged from paper route tips. Jerry told me I learned well and was able to handle his paper route when his knees dislocated. The knees were weak perhaps from fatigue and not enough nourishment to support the hard labor.

Jerry will never forget the time when it was below zero and he had just finished his evening paper route. The wind had been blowing hard and the snow had been drifting high. His hands were numb because of cheap gloves. The family had already sat down to eat because he took longer than normal. He recalls, "It sure could have been nice to get a cup of hot cocoa and some time to thaw out." The young boy was starved and there was one piece of meat left after the rest had their fill. The starving hard working kid, Jerry, asked for it and our apparently less than compassionate Dad said no. Dad indicated to Jerry that little brother Stephen was the "meat eater" and he should have the last piece of meat. According to Jerry, "it was a funny thing because Stephen didn't even ask for it!" That sort of perception of deliberate meanness never went away concerning Jerry's experience at the time.

In Oak Harbor, Washington, where Jerry was stationed at Whidbey Island Naval Air Station, Dad continued his harassment behavior. Jerry has always been an avid non-smoker. Dad kept the house and car full of sickening smoke. As a result, Jerry was asthmatic and highly allergic to the stuff.

Whenever my brother had an asthma attack when he was a teenager it pissed Dad off to no end. He suffered very much in Waukegan where Dad was training boots at the US Naval Training Center in the late 50's. We lived in a little sealed house. Jerry would hang his torso over the side of his cot at night to drain, so he could breathe enough to function the next day. The basement walls were concrete and the windows were un-insulated steel frames that hinged at the bottom. He learned to sleep with the Navy blanket over his head so the air breathed was warm. Jerry left home to join the Navy in 1958. He was just 17 years old, and finally free, at least he thought so at the time. Though he was glad to escape, Jerry held on to a deep desire to love his parents and would continue to make amends and strive to be the son his parents and younger siblings could be proud of and respect.

Brother Jerry, wife Fran and daughter Michelle 1973

Jerry tells the story of Thanksgiving in Oak Harbor, when my younger brother Scott and I were among the guests for his wife Fran's feast. Jerry had Dad at the head of the table. When dinner was finished Steve took Scott out to the car to smoke "you know what." We were relaxing at the table when Dad gave Jerry one of his stupid "dare me" looks and lit up a cigarette at the table. There is karma, however; as Jerry recalls that his lower lip was removed because of *infiltrating squamous* cell cancer. In those days he could have died. The Norfolk Naval Hospital's tumor board contacted him annually for ten years afterwards. He had to answer their letter each time. They were convinced that the cancer was caused by secondary cigarette smoke. It was called smoker's cancer at that time, "damn shitty for a non smoker."

Jerry also remembers when Dad was pissed at him for a past disagreement during a visit at my brother's home in Incline Village, Nevada. At that time, I was at my Brother Dan's house in Tahoe when Dad remarked about the permanent sneer and the look on Jerry's face as a result. Dan and I were disgusted with that remark and shared the story with Jerry later. A couple of years later, Dad's lower lip had been removed for the same cancer. "They did an ugly job on that one," exclaims my brother.

Jerry seemed to feel good about this apparent "payback" resulting from "karma."

Where Jerry is concerned, our father was not an honorable man or a good father. He built the situation to the point where his first born son was a hair away from clubbing him and perhaps fatally. Thank God that he had enough compassion and sense not to go that route and moved on to live a full and productive life.

This was the last review of reasons why Jerry could not respect our father. It is his hope that this account helps us to understand his deep feelings, and that he is given credit for continuing to try until the last family incident in Yakima, Washington, in 1996. After that terrible family encounter, which will not be reviewed in this story, Jerry never turned around and looked back after that day. He also believes that both our parents lost a good friend in Fran, his loving wife. She was the best thing going for their assistance in Tacoma but they were too ignorant to realize the value of the relationship at the time.

It is very sad indeed to write about my dear brother Jerry's experience as a youngster during WWII. His account of that time is highly respected and considered his true beliefs. Some of the dates and times needed to be reconciled with Dad's Naval records. As a young boy, my brother, Jerry, was affected deeply and in a very negative way in his relationship with Dad. Building a bridge to get past the anger and resentment has been extremely challenging for him. Although it is highly unfortunate, I respect Jerry's feelings and pray that he is able to find peace during his remaining years.

As an added tragic note, my brother didn't mention the time in Waukegan just before he entered the Navy that Dad hit him in the head after Jerry was confronted in front of the house by some bullies. He almost took them all on and could have cleaned up since he was so strong. Dad hit his head so hard that it swelled up and we thought he needed medical attention. But Dad was afraid to take him to the hospital. Fortunately, Jerry recovered, but it is my opinion that this incident gave him a severe concussion that needed treatment. I know one thing for sure, as a little kid it hurt me deeply to see this happen. To this day I remember the terrible incident vividly. This horrid event is an example of a man who lived by day as a highly respected war hero training boots at the US Naval Training Center. By night Dad was a mentally ill dangerous man who kept his family in a cage as victims of extreme abuse. None of us would talk about it for fear of being beaten. The US Navy did not see it, nor probably wanted to see it. This was a man who was solely responsible for our welfare, and without him we would have been poor and homeless at the time. We had no choice but to live with him and to avoid his wrath as much as possible. None of us even understood the gravity of the situation until later. Denial certainly helped us survive but all the baggage is clear.

It appears Jerry was not well aware of Dad's experience on the USS Belle Grove. Nor did Dad discuss this part of his war experience very much. My mother mentioned the Belle Grove, but not any details. His old shipmate Charles Minter remembers well, however, and my own digging around certainly shows that this period in the Pacific War was highly secret, so Dad probably didn't write home about it. Dad did mention a time when he was chased into a tomb by Japanese soldiers firing at him. He hid out, and was later rescued by Marines. He said from this moment on he never made fun of his fellow Marines again because they probably saved his life. At that time, navy men did not like be associated with Marines as part of the US Navy. He did mention taking the helm of landing boats to transport our fighting men on shore. But this is about all we know from Dad and the historical records of the USS Belle Grove and accounts by other shipmates on the USS Belle Grove website.

The USS Belle Grove was deployed for 25 months before there was liberty for these sailors following 7 deadly campaigns to take back the islands in the Pacific in preparation for the final defeat and surrender of the Japanese regime. The "bomb" became the only last resort unfortunately because the Japanese culture was highly embroiled in winning at all costs. My brother Jerry, a 30 year Navy veteran and warrant officer himself, calls the war in the Pacific, the "filthy" war. That doesn't mean the war in Europe was clean, it means the Japanese fought and killed like animals, including torture, using swords very effectively to kill instantly or to execute a slow and painful death. The Japanese people of today do not in any way resemble the culture of their WWII legacy. These statements are made with all due respect for the Japanese people and the pain and sacrifice they suffered at the hands of the government during that period.

I do agree with my brother Jerry on how mean and abusive Dad was during my youth as far back as my memory serves. I was scared all the time too.

We never knew when our Dad would go off and start kicking us around for things we didn't really understand at the time. It happened more often when our Mother was nagging him and he had an anxiety attack. Too bad medical research had not progressed enough to provide him with a calming medication. This type of medication helps me a great deal. Wish I didn't have to take it, but the alternative is worse. Living with severe anxiety is an on-going lifelong challenge, but gets easier with age and wisdom. The upside is one's creative side is maximized when "fight" is the response vs. "flight."

It is my prayer and heartfelt hope that my dear brother Jerry can experience peace, real peace during the remaining years of his life. I have forgiven my Dad, and hope Jerry can too. But there is no excuse for any adult, especially a parent, to abuse children the way he did, even though his mental health condition was far from stable and hardly normal. I believe my mother held his hand and kept him calm with her unconditional love right to the end of his life. If you are lucky enough in life to find the right partner, it is she or he who is at your side at the end holding your hand and loving you deeply just like the first day you met and that first special kiss, the one deep long lasting kiss you never forget nor want to end.

Sister Laura turned her life around with faith and hope

I've always loved my only sister Laura. She is 8 years younger than me. For many years it was hard to know how she was doing, but we knew it wasn't going well for her as a kid and as an adult. Laura was abused terribly as a child, especially in her teens, by both parents. She was alone without her big brothers to watch out for her, except little brother Scotty, who cared deeply for her, but was too young to do anything to protect his sister. Dad hurt Laura severely when she was a teen following an abusive neck hold that injured her spine. At age 16, following just too much emotional trauma for one kid, she was sent away to live with Brother Dan and Marcia, where she successfully completed HS and became a responsible adult.

Laura's first marriage lasted long enough to give birth to two beautiful girls, Cari Anna and Tara Leah. She married a second time to Terry and gave birth to a third daughter, Megan Katherine. Terry was a nice guy and a good provider, but abused alcohol to the extent that he was stricken with liver cancer and passed away after over 10 years of marriage. Laura's life really started to go downhill after Terry died and she developed a severe alcoholic problem. She and Megan moved to Oroville, California to start a new life, but both struggled. Laura's injured spine began to cause significant pain and she finally had to have surgery to correct the condition. Alcohol and medications took their toll. Daughter Megan acted out in her teenage years, leaving home often and getting into trouble. Laura worked hard with Megan because she was diagnosed with a behavior disorder and needed specialized help in school, and her work opportunities have been limited.

Finally, Laura had to check into a rehabilitation center in northern California to start a long overdue treatment and recovery process. Megan was left to her own devices for at least a year during this time, living with relatives and friends. While in recovery, Laura started community college taking psychology courses with the goal to become a counselor to support others and to help understand her own life and behaviors better as well. She is a devoted AA member as well as Alanon. Laura is unable to work now because of her disabilities from the spine injury and being diagnosed with PTSD. I respect and adore my sister and see her as a hero for being able to persevere for so many years, start the healing process, and find happiness once again with Tom, her new fiance as of this writing. Laura and Megan now spend quality time together and are becoming closer as friends.

I am so happy to report that Laura has not abused alcohol or drugs for 7 years now. She is happily engaged to a marvelous man named Tom. They live in a mountain town in northern California. Laura is now trying to gain custody of her first grandchild, Dakotah. Her daughter, Megan lives alone in an apartment and is unable to care for her newborn son. We have gotten together twice this summer, once when we were traveling to Reno and again when Laura and Tom came up to the Oregon coast on a camping trip near Newport. Life begins again for my loving Sister Laura! She kept the faith and hope needed to survive and now thrive in a very tough life.

The author, Steve Sparks' reflections

Waiting 40 years to think about my father's war years and my childhood seemed odd at the outset of this journey to research and write a story. I've always wondered about my consistent and troublesome life-long anxiety and drive to succeed. Doing this research has been long overdue, and over a short period of time produced an unexpected positive surprise that changed my mental disposition, allowing the healing process to begin.

Steve Sparks around age 10

I conveniently forgot many things while growing up. The abuse was too difficult and painful to keep on the surface. I buried myself in work and at times alcohol played a role during my free time. Free time and relaxing is not easy, even sleep comes hard for those who suffer from extreme anxiety or PTSD. Alcohol only makes it worse, especially sleeping in a healthy way by going to bed at the right time and waking with body and mind rested. One of the most troublesome problems from my younger years, which occurred while in the US Navy, was completely buried until recently while researching the subject of PTSD and how it affects children of war weary or battle fatigued veterans of any war. You see, my "big secret" has been that my Navy career ended after two years because I was diagnosed with "emotional instability." Today this is a common symptom or one of several criteria that make up the totality of PTSD, which was not apparent or denial took a strong hold on me all these years. This realization and acceptance was a huge moment for me.

I was honorably discharged in August 1965 after two years in the Navy. My Navy experience was very positive and kick-started my career in the telecommunications industry. I became a radioman third class. I graduated from radio school in the top 10% of my class. Bootcamp was a snap because my BMC Dad, Vernon, put me through bootcamp before joining the Navy, including giving me his Naval Regulations Manual to study during the summer of 1963. I was already a "boot" before entering the Navy in July of 1963 at 17 years old. But a problem surfaced unexpectedly while serving at Comsubflot 5 (US Navy Pacific Submarine Fleet Communications Center) in Pearl Harbor, Hawaii.

I was having fun, too much fun, and working 12 on, 12 off, 24 off, 12 on, 12 off with a 72 hour break. Living in Waikiki with 5 other sailors was great too. I would stay on the base during my 12 hour shifts; take off to the beach for romance and surfing during the long weekends. I loved the girls who came over for spring break or after graduating from high school. It was love at first sight just about every other two weeks or so.

My big emotional challenge during that memorable experience in Hawaii was falling in love with a beautiful young lady named Sheryl. She came over for an entire month following her high school graduation. She was tall and slender and very sexy. I met other girls during my stay, but Sheryl was the one that really got my attention. We became intimate right away, and spent the next 30 days or so experiencing a wonderful romance in Hawaii. I loved every moment of her company, and couldn't wait for my next time away from the base to be with her. It was difficult staying on the base while working. I unwisely used my short 24 hour break and took off for Waikiki even though there wasn't a whole lot of time. More often than not I raced down to Waikiki to be with her for a few hours during 12 hour breaks. I didn't want to miss a moment to spend with Sheryl. She was absolutely the best thing that happened to me during my Navy experience in Hawaii. Even surfing took a back seat for awhile. Sleeping became less of a priority as well. Love clearly releases an abundance of energy in a young man. I was already a skinny dude and probably lost another 10 lbs during this high energy period. This experience was simply breathtaking.

One evening, Sheryl and I were really excited about Don Ho's concert at the Hawaiian Hilton right on Waikiki Beach. We found a spot on the beach close to the hotel venue where Don was performing. We couldn't afford to see Don's performance, but it turned out to be one of those spontaneous adventures for two young love birds to take a private seat outside the concert and cuddle in the warm sand. This was definitely a whirlwind romance that took me by surprise, and I'll never know whether it was meant to be a long term relationship. Sheryl was such a beautiful and delightful young lady who came to be part of my life at the time. I had never experienced feelings of this nature before then, but never had the time to really develop our friendship beyond a love affair.

Sheryl finally had to go home. It was dreadful and made my heart sink to say the least, not to mention the thoughts of loneliness that would ensue. I was sure this was real love. We wrote to each other every day. It was hard for me to do anything else. Work and surfing kept me pretty busy. But during off times my mind drifted to Sheryl and the memories of our closeness and the beautiful times we spent together. Each moment with her made me feel complete as a young man. Her praise, friendship, and supportive nature were the best remedies for a young man who rarely experienced love and kindness during the years growing up in a toxic home environment. She was sexy to be sure, but it was much more than that for me. I know from this experience and others that romance is a huge trigger for me. Sex alone does not get me going very much. I needed a soul-mate, a best friend, someone who could care for me with unconditional love, something that would not come to me until much later in life. I had to learn what unconditional love really meant, and trust it completely. I also had to learn that unconditional love is very special and earned in a relationship that has all the characteristics of mutual respect and adoration.

My memories begin to fade, however, as my relationship with Sheryl became serious and we started talking about marriage. I recall writing to Sheryl first and asked her to marry me. Soon later I called her and she accepted. I wanted to bring her over to Hawaii so that we could make a life together. Preparations were made for the wedding, invitations and all the rest. But just before taking leave to return for the wedding, I started to get second thoughts, big second thoughts. These sudden feelings really scared me. I can't remember exactly what was going on in my head, but something was wrong and do not know what precipitated these feelings of fear. Was it possible that my objectivity was taking shape for a change and caused me to look at the relationship in a more realistic way? In hindsight, my emotional disposition was clearly not well suited for launching into a marriage at 19 years of age. I needed much more time to mature and become my own person following the many years of living in a toxic home culture and subjected to abuse. I needed to heal and learn how to build relationships with the opposite sex. I was not equipped at the time to be a good husband and potential father. I know this in my heart now looking back at the time and circumstances.

When I came home on leave to marry Sheryl, after all the preparations were made, it was apparently clear to me when we got together that we had nothing but an Hawaiian romance that was healthy but was not serious enough for a life-long commitment. I was totally confused and anxiety really started to hit me. How could I get out of this and get back to my life in the Navy and in Hawaii where I belong. I wasn't old enough or secure enough to get married. It was at this time that symptoms of PTSD began taking shape in potentially self destructive ways. My memory really starts to fade as the wedding plans and dates are firmed up.

At this time, you could say, "my Dad came to the rescue." He saved me from this marriage by pretending that I was crazy and needed treatment. The big question that lingers to this day is whether or not my crazed effort to get out of this marriage was the right thing to do. Anyway, Dad called for me and broke the news to Sheryl's parents. I chose the coward's route and acted crazy per my Dad's advice. Dad even coached me to put on an act while he was on the phone, yelling, acting out, and crying, etc. He got me out of this situation very effectively. I thanked my father many times after that. But I don't know if it is appropriate to think in terms of "thanking Dad." He orchestrated an escape for me that was less than honorable. This was a very hurtful event for Sheryl and her family. I need to figure out a way to apologize to this family for my behavior even if it is 40 years later.

I believe writing this story is a way for me to apologize to those who were hurt along my troubled journey in life. It is difficult for me to reconcile dragging good and loving people along for a ride on a train destined to crash, leaving everyone behind damaged or hurt emotionally, including me. It would have been a blessing if these kinds of experiences in my life could have somehow been avoided or managed more effectively. But I know the past cannot be changed, and reconciliation may well be a life-time goal for me. There is much more to this traumatic event, so later in this story in a different context, my sister Laura helps me remember the wedding plans from her perspective as a nine year old little girl, which goes a long way to help me understand more clearly what was happening at the time. My memory loss for this period and event suggests it was a highly stressful emotional experience that may have kicked in a chemical reaction in my brain that can be attributed to memory loss.

Once returning to single life serving my country, and enjoying the best shore duty station in the world, the nightmares started, night sweats, lack of sleep, and emotional outbreaks while working the long 12 hour shifts. I was tired and couldn't sleep. I became completely exhausted, and started to act out during my shifts at times. Finally, my Chief took my surfboard away from me, put it in storage, and that really pissed me off to no end. The egotistical jerk (my perspective at the time) put it in plain sight behind a wired tall fence so I could see it every day. My beloved Greg Knoll surfboard that I took with me over to Hawaii was now behind bars and could not be used. That surfboard was my ego and my ticket for picking up beautiful girls on the beach. Surfing gave me a big ego lift along with all the other benefits of being a grown up in the Navy on my own and free of the awful lifestyle left behind in Southern California. I blew up one night and almost kicked the shit out of the 1st class radioman on duty, and told him to fuck off.

Consequently, I was immediately sent to sick bay for a meeting with a psychiatrist. Not too long after that the diagnosis of "emotional instability" came in, and the bottom line was getting kicked out of the Navy. There was really no treatment recommended at that time so it made me feel crazy. I was ashamed and felt like a failure. After all, my dad served honorably and with distinction, a hero from the "Greatest Generation" who survived battle after battle, attack after attack, bombs and more bombs, seeing shipmates killed, and making a huge sacrifice for our country. How would I ever convince my dad that I wasn't a complete fuck up after all, as he said many times? "You are a shit head and will not amount to a tinker's damn." This Navy type slang message from Dad played over and over again as I went through the emotional crisis of separating from the Navy.

Although 40 years later, I am just beginning to remember that right after being diagnosed with "emotional instability" I was reassigned to the USS Coucal (ASR-8) out of Comsubpac. I was stripped of Comsubflot-5 top secret clearance due to my mental condition. The ship was used for submarine tender and salvage and was commissioned in 1942. It was used at the time, 1964-65, as a training ship serving just off shore of the Hawaiian Islands. My brother Jerry helped me to recall this experience recently. On April 22, 2011 we had a long telephone discussion as a follow-up interview to help me with my story. Jerry brought up the USS Coucal, which startled me because my memory appeared to be absent of this event. I have on occasion thought about it, but mostly blocked it from my mind and eventually the experience was completely eliminated from my thought process and was never referenced as something significant in my life.

As my thoughts started returning to the USS Coucal, Jerry was a great resource and I am most grateful for his help in stimulating my memory. It is very scary for me to find out at this point long after the event that my 30 day cruise and experience on the USS Coucal had been completely blocked out of my mind for the most part. I do remember bits and pieces i.e., being on the ship looking at the shore off Makaha Beach and the surfers, feeling very sad about not being back on shore duty enjoying the benefits of surfing. What really happened aboard this ship that led up to my honorable discharge from the Navy, I can't remember. It is completely wiped out! I can't remember anything of any substance at all. I am very anxious to find ways to remember this experience and what happened on board the ship for the 30 days out at sea. I hope it helps me heal from what must have been a highly traumatic time in my life. I subsequently ordered my medical records from the Navy with the hope of finding out more about this experience lost somewhere in my head.

Once receiving my Naval records to review, there was no summary, diagnosis, and treatment of a physical or mental health issue documented from that time. Consequently, I am unable to trace back to any record that might show what happened aboard the USS Coucal. All I know is that my feelings at the time caused me to feel extreme shame and a sense that my life had ended. At age 19 my life was just getting started and on a positive path until this experience hit me like a bolt of lightning. I was working on getting my HS education completed, and thinking about college, and a Navy career in radio communications and electronics. I had no choice but to continue a course of survival of fight or flight. I know fighting was in my blood to be sure. I would go on and win this fight, but not without big scars. I just knew it in my heart and in my gut. My dad was tough and abusive, but he did teach me how to survive.

Reference:
Following service in the Viet Nam War from September 1976 to September 1977, *Coucal* operated from her home port at Pearl Harbor, mainly supporting submarine training. *Coucal* was decommissioned at Pearl Harbor. In April 1990, ex-*Coucal* was sunk in the first PACFLT test of a Tomahawk anti-ship missile, fired from USS *Chancellorsville* (CG-62). Reference: http://en.wikipedia.org/wiki/USS_Coucal_(ASR-8)

The Author's Early Childhood Memories in Context

My earliest memories do confirm my brother, Jerry's account of waiting for Dad at the dock when he returned from one of his cruises during the

Korean War. It is sketchy but I can see the big ship and remember standing with Mother and younger brother Dan looking up at my Dad at the rail waving. I don't see Jerry in my memory but know he was there too. I don't think Dad was very happy for some reason. He just stood there looking out at us, and yes he was big. My Mother did remark how much weight he had gained during the cruise. That memory does stick in my mind. Mother seemed excited but sort of worried about his weight and his disposition. She probably had mixed emotions about his return is my guess based on all the information available up to this point in the story. She was attempting to be positive while being realistic about what to expect in the way of the family reunion that would unfold. Mother had been quite busy during his absence, taking care of the three of us, and waiting for Dad's return as she had done so many times. And mostly disappointment would come to mind when thinking of what was about to occur once they got back together as a family.

The Navy records show that Dad came home on leave on July 1, 1946 to be there for my arrival on July 6th. I know this was a big deal for Dad since he was not home for Jerry's birth. Nothing would keep him from being home for the birth of his second son. Finding this fact in the record made me emotional just thinking about how my Dad probably felt and no doubt how it made my Mother feel at the time. I do have a photo Jerry mentioned earlier of all three of us shortly after I was born. This is the photo where Jerry said he felt scared. Believe we were at a park somewhere near Oakland, California, my birth place.

My sister Laura and brothers often told me that I was abused the most, but my memory seems to fail me often. There are some things I remember, but most memories start to pick up pretty good around age 5 and starting after 1951. I do know that I suffered polio when I was two years old, but have no memory of what happened. The story goes, however, that polio became an epidemic around that time, and apparently I was exposed somehow to the virus and it struck my left side. My jaws locked up so they had to place some sort of brace in my mouth to aid in feeding me. My left side starting from my face down my left arm was paralyzed from polio.

I know my Dad was scared, so I'm told, and cried a lot. He thought it was his fault that this happened for some reason. He blamed himself and my mother tried to convince him otherwise. The March of Dimes helped a great deal to pay for my recovery over the next few years as I learned how to use my left arm again and to move my jaw. I did not have severe polio, but it was bad enough to delay my development as a kid and made me feel insecure and not as strong as other kids for a long time. My left arm has always been weak with muscle loss and my left chest and breast area was affected. I became self conscious of not having a macho chest as I grew older. I wore t-shirts quite a bit and put my right hand under my left arm to cover the dent in my chest. My jaw was crooked from the experience and I had bucked teeth. Other than that, I was probably one of the most handsome and sexiest guys around, at least girls thought so. Guys, including my brothers and Dad would make fun of me. Kids can be cruel but you would think parents would be nicer about things like this. But my Dad's behavior would suggest that he would accept nothing less than 100% performance from any one of us, even with a disability or two. After all Dad was a hero who survived all kinds of bad things and observed many more awful events and had to keep going no matter what, so guess he believed his sons had to do the same. In a way, forcing me to believe I was a typical kid was an advantage. Treating me normal was not a bad thing. I believe, through understanding the work my wife Judy does with special needs children, that the more typical kids can be treated the easier it is for them to assimilate and to make adjustments to adapt to their own limitations. My parents may have been using this technique with me as a common sense approach, but could have taken it too far at times. After all they were not educated on matters of child rearing and parenting.

My brother Dan and I were always involved in different kinds of capers together. We were very close and still are to this day. Dan is my best friend. We talk every week, sometimes several times. We don't engage in capers anymore, but a couple of stories are worth mentioning.

I loved saving stamps and pursuing it as a hobby. I believe Dan came up with the idea that we should go to the stamp store and steal stamps and hide them for awhile, and retrieve them later when everybody dismissed the crime. The story goes that we took a bunch of stamps from our local stamp store and put them into a box and found a perfect spot to bury them next to a barn. I decided to put our name and address on the box so we could identify it later. Dan didn't know it. When we buried the stamps, I turned around and went back and put a stick in the ground so as to remember where we buried the stamps. A few days later someone else dug up the box, discovered the stamps, and called Mother. Dan and I had to return the stamps to the store and apologize all over the place. Dan has not forgiven me to this day for being as stupid as to leave our name and address on the box. He was right. Dan was potentially good at crime but not me. I would get caught every time. This insecurity about not being able to get away with criminal behavior really helped me in my life.

Another crime we did get away with and to this day don't know why is when we put on long coats as young teens and entered a 7-Eleven to steal wine. We actually succeeded in putting Ripple Wine bottles in our coats and walking out. This was another criminal plot my brother Dan put together, but this time we succeeded. I remember getting drunk with him drinking that rotten wine, Ripple shit. Still this successful crime did not get me going on doing anything like it again. I don't remember participating with my brother in breaking the law again.

Our time in Minnesota brings back memories of my Dad's drinking and unstable behavior. He had nightmares often and woke up in the middle of the night yelling "Japs, Japs, Japs." He punched a few holes in the ceiling at that time. One time at the dinner table he seemed to be so pissed about something that he took his big right hand and crunched salt and pepper shakers into dust on the table. I can also remember him punching the toilet and breaking it apart, cutting a tendon in his hand. Dad was huge and

The author washing Ralph c. 1960

strong. Just like his old shipmate from the Belle Grove, Charles Minter said, "his arms were long, real long."

We would typically launch into a defensive position to protect our heads when Dad was mad or when it appeared that he was about to go off. I remember clearly how we put our arms over our heads often when he was around. Sometimes he would come into the house really pissed off and go after us and beat the shit out of each of us. Dan and I were always getting into trouble in Minnesota. Dad drank quite a bit during this time while he was at the Federal Correctional Institution in Sandstone, Mn about 60 miles north of the Twin Cities where our family lived.

Our grandpa Art and grandma Mildred would come for visits at times, and he and his dad really got into the booze big time. Dan and I got into big time trouble when we took his whiskey bottle and tossed it so he couldn't drink anymore. That was a huge mistake! Boy did we get our asses kicked that time.

My parents didn't get along very well in Sandstone. My mother hated it there and wanted to return to California, so she was in a constant nagging and complaining mode for two years before he gave up and got transferred back to Terminal Island Federal Correctional Institution near Long Beach. Mother would not stop whining, complaining and blaming. To this day, I hate whining, complaining and blaming.

I'm a strong believer in doing something to solve a problem and looking at alternatives rather than making emotional decisions. Although not perfect in my life on this subject, I've done so to the extent that at least I've minimized risk to some degree by thinking this way. No whining! Too many mistakes are made when one is preoccupied with this sort of behavior rather than looking at the issues and concerns and trying to isolate the problem needed to be addressed, then looking at potential solutions starting with the ones that make the most sense and have the best return on investment. WOW! Guess I learned something of value since it has helped me in my career and in my life as a whole.

I know Dan and I loved Minnesota. The girls liked us because we were from California. Guess there was something about California that made them feel like we were celebrities of sorts. I played sports and felt pretty good about myself most of the time. I remember my first sexual encounter in Minnesota as well. This is the one encounter that happens out in the barn with all the animals between a girl and boy with raging hormones.

Dan and I really picked up on fishing in the Sandstone River. We would often hike down to the Sandstone Dam and fish. I remember the time Dan hooked a huge fish and lost it. The one that got away is all we could talk about for years. That day the black flies were so bad we had to run back through the woods home fast to get away from them.

Sadly, I recollect our loving dog, Ralph. Having a pet was such a good thing in our life. I have a photo of me with Ralph in a tub out back of our house. We lived next to the main highway so always tried to be careful with Ralph, but one night Ralph wanted to go out and it was cold as hell that winter. So I insisted on letting him out in the cold by himself. We found Ralph the next morning frozen dead off to the side of the road. We heard the truck going by the night before so had a feeling Ralph was hit.

Dad was pretty brutal in Minnesota. He was constantly telling us we were no good and would never amount to anything in life. I'm sure it bothered us a great deal but didn't hold us back. It seemed like we developed a "we'll show this asshole" attitude about his constant ranking us down behavior. Dan and I were buddies and we stuck together, even to this day it is the same. We have a bond that can never be broken. Jerry didn't have anyone to protect or support him, so having each other was a huge advantage living in a toxic environment.

Our favorite and most memorable experience in Minnesota was staying on Uncle Harry's farm outside of Ascov, Minnesota a short drive from Sandstone. Two summers in a row Dan and I could go there for about 30 days and work. We worked hard making hay and milking cows and shoveling shit. We were treated well and boy did they feed us. They only had an outhouse and little plumbing inside, but it was a real character building experience and we felt loved by Uncle Harry and Aunt Leona. I can remember we hated to go home when the time came.

Friday nights in downtown Sandstone was a treat for sure. Everybody came to town on Friday night for football etc., and just hang out with friends. This experience was healthy good stuff at that time in a small town culture. It just doesn't get any better than that.

Moving back to California was the shits. None of us wanted to do it, but Mother was relentless, so Dad finally gave in. I remember the trip back to California in the hot summer was terrible. Sitting in the back seat of the car knowing my Dad's long arms could reach us easily, and they did, was scary. Mother continued to whine and complain and blame, reminding Dad of all the rotten shit he put us all into with his decisions. Dad was able to get his frustrations out by hitting us with those long arms and big hands while we acted out in the back seat. While it wasn't the right thing to do, Dad probably thought it would be better to beat us than my mother, who really deserved it more. Considering she was a woman with barely a 7th grade education, she had a motor mouth that would not stop, and all that came out was negative, nothing positive that deserves some recognition. Some of that booze my Dad was hiding in the car somewhere would have been a blessing, except no one but Dad could drive, so he stayed away from the stuff too.

I believe all of this so far begs the question of how it affected my own disposition as my teen years advanced. I was feeling more and more insecure as time went by, wondering about what was next, and who our new friends would be, and how we would fit in, and what my parents would end up doing, and where we would live. There was some excitement about returning to Southern California at that time, getting back to school, and meeting new girls especially. I had lots of goals and my thoughts were often of the future, leaving home and being on my own. I wanted out of this chaotic and unstable toxic home life. I was nervous very nervous most of the time. I believe the early stages of PTSD and unstable behavior started to kick in at that time. At age 14 or so, I felt exhausted and confused, without direction, and not knowing whether my parents really cared about us at all.

Jerry was gone now. So, it was me, Dan, and Laura. Laura was quiet most of the time until later. She was just a little girl and highly resilient as kids go at that age. Things would catch up with Laura when she became a teenager after I left home. Dad was able to transfer to the Federal Correctional Institution on Terminal Island near Long Beach. We lived in a couple of different rental homes in the Torrance and Carson areas where I attended Stephen M. White Junior HS. I really got into surfing around this time, which helped my ego a great deal. I learned how to surf at Redondo Beach around 1960 and hung around with the surf crowd. I loved the girls from Palos Verdes! They were sexy and rich. I really didn't think I had a chance with any of them, but sure dreamed about it.

Dan wasn't a surfer, but hung out with guys who loved the beach too and who also loved to pick fights with others. Dan was a fighter. He liked to kick ass all the time. The only ass he couldn't kick was mine. But my brother saved me plenty of times from gangs of guys who got into fights at the beach. He and his friends would show up and clean everybody out and he often saved my ass. I don't think fighting was something I liked all that much, but lots of guys at that time were into it big time. I tried to stay on the positive side of most things, a romantic so to speak. Even to this day, my brother Dan wants to kick ass, but he is getting too old now. I try to coach him a bit and remind him that he is in no position to kick anybody's ass. I don't believe Dan listens to me very much, but do try to pass a little wisdom on to him. He is my little brother.

The worst memory Dan and I have is when we hitchhiked to Long Beach one day and got a ticket for jay walking. When we went home and told Dad and showed him our ticket, he freaked out. He accused us of ruining his career as a correctional officer and would kill us for sure. He chased us around the kitchen table and was so angry it scared the living shit out of both of us. My mother stood by and said nothing, allowing this to happen. To this very day the memory sticks in my mind as the epitome of mental and physical abuse from Dad. Give me a break, a "jay walking ticket" ruining my Dad's career in law enforcement and correctional work? One thing for sure, neither one of us ever got busted for anything, but we did get away with breaking the law a few times. We were lucky to say the least, but our Dad had nothing to worry about, and certainly his behavior was way over the top.

I do recognize now, however, that Dad was having an anxiety attack, and something this small, as in a "jaywalking" infraction, is symptomatic of the behavior of a person suffering from PTSD. It doesn't take much. But this is the kind of experience that sticks with kids and does not enhance their image of parenting or modeling constructive behavior. You are left with a sense of loss and confusion and no direction as a kid. It models an uncontrolled behavior that could be transferred to a child who might think it is okay to have a ridiculous outburst like this. "Ridiculous" was a popular word in our family. It's a word that was used probably 10 times or more a day, especially by Mother. Another highly popular statement was, "he don't." Dan and I with the help of school and friends finally broke this terrible use of words. Dan and I became obsessed in using words effectively and in the right context.

Little Bro Danny helps me to Remember!

I called Danny as we approached the Grand Canyon area to spend the night in Flagstaff, Arizona. Judy and I were on the 2nd week of our summer 2011 road trip. Danny once again reminded me of my troublesome memory repressions. I had been convinced for many years that we visited the Grand Canyon as kids while on a trip back to California when Dad was transferred to a new Navy duty station and reaching the end of his naval career. This was not the case to be sure. Danny told me the story that we were very excited about going to the Grand Canyon, but Dad was tired and anxious at the time, including being mean and abusive as hell. His long arms and huge hands were very effective in reaching to the back seat of the car where we were all sitting and beating the shit out of us with a surprise attack any moment. We kept our arms over our heads most of the time to protect ourselves; a permanent hand/arms over heads position worked effectively to mitigate blows to the head.

Mother was constantly whining, complaining, and blaming about everything that could be considered a negative experience in her life, including this trip to California. My mother was never happy about anything. As the story goes, Dad finally decided we were not going to the Grand Canyon, and that was final. As Danny recalled and described it to me, he had a complete temper tantrum, ran to the car and slammed the door so hard it broke the back right window. Fortunately, the windows were always open in the extremely hot weather, so when the parents walked back to the new '57 Chevy, the broken window was not noticed. The problem with all of this is that I don't remember a thing about the experience, nothing whatsoever. It is even more concerning to me now because of my age of 11 at the time, my memories should be quite clear, just like they are for bro Danny. When we arrived in California, Dad discovered the broken window and thought it happened along the way on the bad roads, so he got it fixed. Danny got away with this one like lots of pranks. He was smart and kept his mouth shut, a smart move most of the time.

Yet another example of memory loss consistent with PTSD symptoms is making writing this story both frustrating and challenging. There are vague memories of this trip back to California following my Dad's stint at the Great Lakes Naval Training Center near Chicago, Illinois. Danny's memory is now critical to helping me remember events accurately and correctly. My brother became an extension of my brain while writing this story, allowing me to piece together my life to around age 11. Things are now getting a little clearer, and the dates and times are beginning to connect. But the memory suppression is becoming the most worrisome aspect of my desire to capture the past and to reconcile all the apparent mental and physical abuse. My mental disposition was clearly affected differently than Danny who remembers everything, including all the details as if it happened yesterday. My brother was able to compartmentalize and cope far better than me, and therefore kept his mind clear of bad things while preserving his memories of our childhood even under the worst conditions.

We can easily conclude that coping skills are different for everyone. I coped by suppressing events, and Danny coped well by being more objective and mature about most situations we confronted. With the temper tantrum example, he was much better at expressing his emotions than me, releasing his anger, and actually getting past it. Getting past my anger has been a more recent experience in my life, long after the suppressed events occurred. I chose to hide it or suppress my memory rather than deal with it right away and get past it. I believe Danny's approach is a much healthier way, but it doesn't make him any better off from all the toxic living than me. He still has big baggage to carry around and is in denial most of the time, suggesting that he is stronger than all of us. And as a result he doesn't have as many residual effects from our abusive childhood, so he believes, but not so in reality.

Speaking of Danny, I must describe this character, who is my loving brother and close friend. As much as I love my brother, he pisses me off most of the time. He believes he is the smartest guy in the room most of the time, if not all of the time. Danny is an instructional sort of guy. You name the topic and he knows more about it than anyone else in the world. There is no one person, absolutely no one who can compete with his knowledge about all things and everything. Danny is about 6 ft tall, and a skinny dude. He looks pretty healthy and has the same weight now that he had when he was 18 or so, 165 lbs. I used to weigh 165-170 lbs during my teens and life in the Navy, but it didn't take long before weight started to become a challenge. Danny, on the other hand, does everything he possibly can to gain weight to no avail. This alone is enough to piss me off and most other people as well. Bro Danny looks like Ted Turner with his stash, but with more hair. Having more hair is another reason to be pissed off at

Danny. Everyone else in their 60's is getting fat, ugly, and losing their hair, but Danny has somehow been passed up. Guess it is the Lakota Native

American blood lines that help him more than the rest of us. Our great grandmother Sparks from North Dakota was half Lakota, making us 1/16 following the ancestry tree.

**Brother Danny, circa December 1984, in Shell uniform
with his new baby daughter, Adria**

Danny is a highly successful businessman from Nevada. He has owned a very popular full service auto operation for 25 years, and has done really well with the business. Of course, at times it has been a challenge, but for the most part Danny has made it big with hard work, smarts and passion. Danny and I are fortunate to have completed college on our own. He's a tough guy too. Even now at our advancing age he thinks he can kick everybody's ass easily with his "Chuck Norris" training of long ago. Even when we were kids he could kick everybody's ass except me. I think he just scared the shit out of his peers on the street and at the beach. I know he protected me all the time, and I owe my life to him. Fortunately, Danny can't kick anybody's ass anymore these days, and I have to remind him of it all the time.

Danny has been married to Marcia for 43 years this month. They have three children, Jeremy, Branden, and Adria. I love his kids and remain close to them after all these years. Our summer 2011 road trip included visiting with all of them at different times. Adria just became engaged to a wonderful French guy named Jonathan, who really has the smarts, good looks and passion to do well in life, including being a good romantic as in French. I am very close to my brother's family. Although I love his wife Marcia, and have known her since she was 15, I don't think she has ever liked me all that much, but I know she loves me. The kids call me "Uncle Stevie." This is my brand, the one and the only Uncle Stevie, their favorite uncle to be sure.

In my opinion, Danny has done much better in later life coming to terms with his painful childhood and taking the high road with our parents. Still, the experiences of living in a toxic home while growing up present personal challenges just like the rest of us. His excellent work ethic and hyper-vigilant behavior is a great match for success. My research so far has been both interesting and helpful to him and he supports my work 100%. Danny is a huge contributor to this story since his memory serves him well and provides me with the editing and accuracy so critical to writing a successful nonfiction story. Danny hugged me for at least 2 minutes when we left Reno this time and it made me emotional. After all the shit and more bullshit we exchange during our visits and talks, the closeness we feel toward each other is special.

My Little Sister Laura remembers "the wedding that didn't happen"

Laura remembers all of the excitement when I came home to marry my loving fiancée, Sheryl. Laura thought Sheryl was so beautiful and the wedding planning was like a fairy tale to her at nine years old. Laura loved playing with her Barbie and Ken dolls, imagining beautiful and perfect lives for them! Laura fantasized, "Here is my big brother Stephen with his beautiful fiancée, real life Barbie and Ken…!"

Laura was especially excited because Sheryl asked her to be one of her bridesmaids, the "junior bridesmaid" along with her younger sister.

Although Laura doesn't remember her sister's name, she remembers playing together at the parent's home in the San Fernando Valley.

As Laura recalls, Sheryl, her Mom, Dad and sister lived in a beautiful Spanish adobe style home in the San Fernando Valley. The home was surrounded by perfect manicured landscaping with gorgeous old trees, flowering shrubbery, and perfect green lawns. All the homes on the street were different, however, large and elegant. The windows were round with iron bars, ceilings with open beams like the old Spanish California missions that Mother insisted we tour in our family travels.

Laura recalls further, Sheryl and her mom were going to sew the dresses for the girls in the wedding party. They were ivory linen with ruffles and empire style waist. Sheryl's sister and Laura were fitted several times, she remembers. It was so much fun and excitement for her.

It hurts me to think about how my sister was so very disappointed when the wedding didn't happen after all. She remembers Dad yelling at me the night before and all the chaos going on at our home in Gardena, California.

The sad part is that I don't remember a thing about this event, except the larger and overwhelming torture of trying to figure a way out of the marriage. Whether this marriage was right or wrong I will never know, but will try to reconcile this hurtful experience in the context of finding peace in what happened. I apparently hated myself for the cowardly act of backing out of this marriage and using my father to help me confront the family. I was a "runaway groom" to be sure. I don't know how this event affected Sheryl and her family, but it must have been tragic. I now know it was tragic for me since I suffered a memory loss for many months following this experience until finally coming home again from the Navy to start my life as a civilian. I will make every attempt to find Sheryl and apologize deeply for not being strong enough to confront the issue directly with her and her family. It is clear to me now that my behavior, although connected to emotional instability and PTSD symptoms, was inexcusable. My memory is so foggy on this period of time that I can't even remember Sheryl's last name! I am so ashamed and know this experience will haunt me forever. Finally, in terms of parental behavior in this circumstance, I would never dream of engaging in this type of intervention with any of my children, never! Where was my good character? Where was my mind? Where was my strength when needed the most? At age 18 or 19, I was clearly in need of appropriate guidance from a role model that did not come my way at the time.

The other highly troublesome memory is shortly after I returned from the Navy and lived at home for a few months. Dad had an anxiety attack about something, and came into our room waving a gun at Dan and me. Talk about scary! Shit, Dad was really off his rocker at this moment. What in God's name was he thinking about by pulling out his gun in some kind of crazy rationalization that somehow waving and pointing a gun at his boys would produce a positive result, or even close to it. This was so nuts even my Mother, who normally steps back, held him off this time. She may have intervened at the right time and saved us from being wounded or worse, killed, ruining the rest of his and everyone's life from that point on. After all this we didn't need a homicide investigation in our home and have Dad taken off to jail for the rest of his life, not to mention the waste of all the potential in the room considering what his sons accomplished in life with or without him guiding us appropriately or effectively in a consistent, thoughtful, and loving way.

I was finally able to move to Hermosa Beach after this incident, and get on with my life. Free again, but not without life continuing to happen with one challenge after another. I had goals, however, big goals. The first big decision was to not stay in Hawaii when discharged from the Navy. To this day I believe this was one of my most important choices. A remarkable adult thinking model occurred for me in making the move to come home. My own conclusion was that my chances of getting a good job and getting back into school to finish K-12 and go on to college would be far easier than staying in Hawaii and pursuing a life of a homeless surf bum. Really, that was my thinking even though the thought of going home was not pleasant knowing what kind of reception was waiting for me and knowing living at home for awhile would be necessary.

The first surprise of my post Navy job hunting came when interviewing with General Telephone in Redondo Beach, California. I passed all the tests and had more than adequate qualifications using my radio and electronics training and experience in the Navy as a big advantage to add value as a new employee working in the telephone industry. After all the tests and interviewing I was called to the HR office in Redondo Beach to find out when to report for work. School would be first at General Telephone. I would train for a position of teletype technician supporting the large base of TWX customers in the Los Angeles area. I was so excited about the thoughts of getting on with my career and life, including more school. It was hard to hold back dancing all the way to this meeting. Then the bad news came.

A security and background check showed that I was diagnosed by a Navy MD with "emotional instability" and there was a code on my DD214 that I was completely unaware of at the time. This was a huge let down and started reinforcing my original belief that my life would be ruined and destined to be poor with this sort of mental disorder on the record. I really had not taken the time to understand how this note on my DD214 would affect my chances of employment. The Navy did not have a treatment plan other than kicking me out on the street, and adding to the problem they were required to make a notation of the "reason for discharge" in my record for the world to see. My thought was that an "Honorable Discharge" and continued Navy reserve status for the next 4 years would pave the way for a clean transition to civilian life, and give me a jump start because of my outstanding performance, including technical vocational training, for the two years spent in the Navy. I was shocked and depressed to say the least. This event really caused me to become extremely anxious, including loss of sleep and tremors. After a few weeks I did get back up from the floor and headed out again on a tip that Western Union was looking for teletype operators. I was a high speed teletype operator in the Navy, achieving close to 90 words a minute.

Once again, the excitement was back in full force. I passed all the tests at Western Union and got hired. I was sent to school for three months in downtown Los Angeles on 714 South Flower Street where my career in the telecommunications industry begin. Hot damn, thank you God for sticking with me! I moved on with complete confidence and enthusiasm because work and school would become the best therapy possible for my mental disorder. I needed to be surrounded by all things positive and positive people who were good mentors and enthusiastic about life and careers. I was just like a dog when getting praise, the more the better, and "praise" was my treat. My life as a kid did not include a whole lot of praise or reinforcement. Western Union picked me up so much that I quickly finished the five credits needed to graduate from HS and enroll at Harbor Junior College in San Pedro, California. College was excellent therapy as well. I wanted to learn everything, especially get passed the bad grades in HS to move forward in college, and focus on interpersonal communications skills, including writing and public speaking. My goal was to move into sales as soon as a position at Western Union became available, but knew well that I had to become much more effective at writing and speaking intelligently. But I always loved selling, and knew somehow this would be in the mix during my career. I was also thrilled with the whole idea of learning about technology at a very exciting time in the early days of information technology evolution, from the mid 60's forward.

Before moving on with the story, it is healthy to again acknowledge my "big secret." I decided when not getting the job at General Telephone for the reason of "emotional instability" on my Navy record would never ever come up in any discussion. My story would center on getting a "hardship discharge" due to severe family issues at home. It was far too risky at the time to share this kind of perceived damaging information with anybody anytime, even those close to me. I felt that my entire life and career, including earnings potential would be compromised if this got out. Consequently, I learned how to compartmentalize the diagnosis, put it away for good, and pretend there was never any mental problem on my part. On the surface, this worked as long as my ego was fed appropriately and adequately with my life moving along at a rapid rate, including an abundance of positive, ego building stimuli. As a leader, even observing and experiencing the success of others working for or with me provided the same ego building fuel. I thrived in a team environment working around professional people with lots of intensity and a drive to succeed. The down times, although not often, considering work, school, falling in love, etc., were difficult. Sleep was hard to come by, relaxing was difficult, and there was always a throbbing sort of uncomfortable feeling in my chest. It was always there, and never went away until later in life. Moderate use of alcohol was helpful, and occasional use of marijuana seemed cool at the time, but I now realize how unacceptable this behavior was at the time. My priorities of work and school were so strong that I needed to be in control of everything all the time. My work ethic kept my use of alcohol in check during this period, and the use of marijuana became part of my past. Nothing would get in the way of achieving the high goals set for myself.

A highly structured life worked well to keep me grounded. As my age advanced and I became more secure with work and the discipline of school, alcohol became more of an off-times habit; I developed an "it must be 5 o'clock somewhere" attitude. There was no other medication or treatment available at that time, and I did not want to reveal my "big secret."

Western Union became my favorite ego building pastime during daytime hours. My enthusiasm and intensity was a welcome sign in this "green eyeshade" world of career secure people who loved waiting for retirement to roll around. I loved to "stir the pot" and get those around me excited about everything, making a big deal about everything, celebrating success at every opportunity. Higher management recognized at that time that change was mandatory for Western Union to succeed in a soon to be highly competitive world of telecommunications. Western Union offices were closing at a rapid rate, the telegram was being replaced with Mailgram, TWX, Telex, and computerized message switching networks (store and forward x.25 technology reference: http://en.wikipedia.org/wiki/X.25) replacing the old step and manual switching systems of the day. Westar I was launched, kicking off the space age of telecommunications and broadcasting, bringing the cost of infrastructure down along with the cost of written communications and increasing the speed of transmission exponentially at that time. The perfect world for Steve Sparks was to hide his mental instability disorder and to succeed as a professional salesman in the booming information technology business. I knew exactly where and how to get there! But I am unable to explain how I knew this. Excellent sales professionals are considered half crazy anyway, so this could have been my subtle thinking about the subject.

I became extremely motivated and the wind was at my back most of the time. I struck gold at the right time and knew it, so believe it was time to go in for the kill and never look back. Nights were all about school, and learning to be an effective communicator was a huge priority. I had good mentors who coached me and critiqued me daily on how to become a professional, a top professional to be sure. I wanted to be the best, the very best at everything I did, especially in relationships with customers, addressing their needs and responding with solutions to problems. Building strong relationships with peers and customers became an obsession with me. I loved it, every minute of it, and could not get enough of it. Most of my co-workers, except bosses, could not keep up with me. My superiors enjoyed my "kick ass and take names" work ethic, while my peers resented me. Customers loved me and my sales performance became exceptional over a very short period of time. My boss started giving me assignments where others had failed and thought my "get it done" attitude and enthusiasm would set an example. And it did set the right example of solving problems for customers rather than giving excuses. I worked internally to fix our weak links and go back to customers with solutions in terms of applications or a technical fix. I was able to get team members to understand what customers were demanding and thinking and what we needed to do to succeed. I managed to learn how to get team members and support groups to buy into my strategies to win customers back. It was all a game to me and we were winning. I loved winning and hated losing. But things evened out a bit when I fell in love with my first wife; at least I thought it was love.

My brother Dan and his girlfriend Marcia (later married) introduced me to Lillian at Hermosa Beach one day in the summer of 1967, a perfect day indeed. Lillian was a beautiful and sweet Italian girl, just 17, heading into her senior year at Carson High School. I was attracted to her right away. She was a little shy but was a kind and thoughtful person. I like that in women and still do today. We hit it off right away in fact. She even got caught in the rip tide while we were wading in the water. I sort of saved her from getting pulled under. What luck to have right away after meeting a very attractive and likable young woman!

Lillian and Marcia had been friends since they were very small and remain close friends to this day. I had heard about her Italian family and all the closeness and fun they had together. I loved the idea of meeting a relatively normal, close and loving family. She was from exactly the right combination of good looks and a loving family for me at that time. A close family was the last thing I could talk about in my life. Besides, my brother Dan and Marcia were both close to Lillian's family and adored them as well. What a nice introduction to a new girl friend and a family to enjoy, and love to go with it. I could not wait to meet them, and experience my first Italian dinner with the entire clan. I kept hearing about the cooking and fun family gatherings that had been only in my dreams.

Lillian and I hit it off. I loved her family and always felt so good in their company. This was the kind of family I've always dreamed of. No, they weren't perfect, but there was a bond and love between all of them that I had never been exposed to before. I really didn't understand all of this until later in life. At that time, I was still too much into myself and my career to really think about or appreciate enough the dynamics of a loving family and what it really meant. I believe there was fear on my part to really let go and capture this wonderful family culture as my own. I felt at times that I might not be good enough or did not deserve the kind of closeness all these folks felt for each other, and distrusted what appeared to be a genuine feeling toward me as Lillian's new boyfriend.

I shared everything with Lillian except my "big secret." And that is probably what really held me back from trusting the situation completely. It was so important to me not to compromise my macho self and to avoid admitting to any mental disorder, that I did not fully embrace Lillian's family culture. I didn't deserve it...

I felt my relationship with Lillian would help ground me and give me the extra discipline needed to achieve my career and educational goals. Her family made me feel secure and grounded as well. It was a far different feeling than when I visited with my own parents where I was instantly reminded of the toxic aspects and how much I detested the kind of life style of abuse and hate of where I came from. Of course, my parents ended up moving to Tacoma, Washington so my dad could take a new job at the Federal Correction Institution on McNeil Island across from Tacoma.

In the fall of 1967, Lillian became pregnant with our first child, Deanna. We were married in February, 1968. I felt in love with Lillian and wanted to be a responsible adult about our situation. I had a good start with my career and in getting myself down the road with college. I know a certain amount of anxiety and pressure was on my mind; I became extremely nervous at times. I should have been a more responsible adult and safer about our relationship. I was the adult after all. This huge lesson stays with me today when talking to young people. But at the same time I would not go back and change a thing. Life does not work that way. You take responsibility and do the best you can to make it all work out. As the reader will find out I didn't do so well during this period of my life on the personal and family side of things. It was a very regretful period and lives on and with me today.

Deanna arrived on July 15, 1968. I was with Lillian for her birth, and still have a scar on my left hand where she held my hand so tight that the skin broke open from her nails digging in. That scared me a bit because it showed how painful giving birth was while being a wonderful life experience at the same time. Deanna was a beautiful baby and healthy. Lillian and I were both very proud. We took Deanna home to our new apartment in Redondo Beach to start our new life as a family.

It didn't take long for me to jump right back into my career and to continue school. I was so obsessed with work and school that it got my attention at times. While my friends were out surfing or hanging out somewhere, I was either working or studying. I accepted responsibility as a new father, but couldn't stand the thought of failing and not being able to take care of them. Lillian had just a HS education, so it was of paramount importance for me to succeed in my career and to complete my education. I was not the kind of Dad that spent every moment with the baby, but did enjoy watching Deanna grow and took her to the beach and other places during the little free time I earned. Lillian was a wonderful mother, and she had lots of support from her own family. She was very encouraging to me in my career and in getting through college. I regretfully admit that work and school were higher priorities than my family to me at the time. I did not find a good balance. It was all or nothing when it came to fighting for survival. I was still in the "I'll show them" mindset, and refused to work toward a better balance between work, school, and family.

Lillian tolerated my obsessive behavior knowing that there was a lot at stake, but not realizing how my behavior was the beginning of becoming more and more distant and less loving toward Lillian and my family as a whole. Deep inside I also resented having to take on so much responsibility much earlier than expected. It was hard, very hard. This is one of those moments in my life that gives me pause to think about young people and the consequences of starting a family too early. The pressures of work and school and family caused my anxiety level to go through the roof and period of angers began to surface. I couldn't stand the thought of failing, not this time, not any time, not again. Alcohol, surfing, and hanging out with the guys after work sometimes gave me relief. Was I trying to escape? Was "flight" behavior beginning to take shape in my life?

I continued to enjoy the many weekend visits with Lillian's family. It was always a riot. Lillian's father was a big Italian dude who loved whiskey and water chasers, and all of us joined him in the kitchen. Ed Castagnola was a tug boat engineer and operator for the Wilmington Transportation Company. He was a man's man to be sure. He loved his boys and we all drank together on the weekends while waiting for the delicious dinner, usually an Italian feast. And we did get drunk and carried away at times. We even had disagreements and yelling matches, but there was never any violence like I used to experience at home. They always settled down and hugged each other. There was an abundance of love and closeness in Lillian's family that was very special to me.

I came home one day and announced to Lillian that a promotion was offered me to become a sales manager for Western Union in Detroit, Michigan. Of all places, we remarked at the time. Who in their right mind would move to Detroit, Michigan? I explained to Lillian that this was called "paying dues" in the business, especially at Western Union. Your first assignment when moving up in the ranks was to be sent to the worst God awful place they could find to receive the very best on-the-job training. I explained that this was my big chance to move up into senior management far sooner than expected, and big things were planned for me going forward. Lillian again was very supportive and gave me her blessings to take on the challenge. And it was a challenge, a big one at that. I was hardly prepared for a management level responsibility at such a young age of 23-24, entirely too young to be a sales manager in some strange city far away from my favorite surf spot, 22nd Street in Hermosa Beach. To top it off I would remind myself of the earlier diagnosis of "emotional instability" that ended my naval career and wondered if I would be taking on too much, too early. But the desire to succeed and the potential rewards could launch my career to new heights.

Lillian became pregnant with Bianca early in 1970, right around the time that all the career changes started taking place. Having a second child was part of our plan. We wanted Deanna to have a sister or brother to grow up with. But now it was even more apparent that moving up in my career was critical to our family, and these opportunities do not come up very often. I had a chance to go into a new area and build up a sales department that was failing in meeting expectations. This would be my first "turn-around" assignment. Frankly, I was scared of what to expect and whether my experience and skill sets to this point would help me succeed. My gut told me to do it, but from an intellectual point of view, I thought my superiors were nuts sending a kid in to do a man's job. Rather, I thought, being nuts myself is probably why they are sending me to fix it. My mentors at Western Union figured I was some sort of miracle worker at the time, so there was a lot to live up to. The expectations were very high. I would try to use my emotional instability problem as an advantage, but that's my secret weapon. All the anxiety and nervous energy did work to my advantage most of the time. It gave me the mental strength to stay steps ahead of everybody else.

Leaving Lillian at home for awhile, I took off for Detroit in the spring of 1970. Western Union put me up in a temporary living apartment to start my new job and to look for a home for my family. That first weekend in Detroit was lonely. I was trying to figure out why I would do such a stupid thing moving all the way here to this city and away from my comfort zone in southern California. I think other people thought I was stupid too. But in my mind many opportunities to succeed are lost when you don't take a calculated risk. I believe to this day that when a door opens, go through it, but go through it in a calculated goal-oriented way. Have a plan and dream of a successful outcome. I remind myself often, even today, that dreams come first and without a dream and a mindset and passion for success, do not proceed with any new endeavor. Adjustments along the way are always necessary, but one needs to take the initiative to move forward before anything good happens.

I just barely made it home for Bianca's birth on October 10, 1970. She was just a sweetie and a beautiful baby just like her sister Deanna. Although fathers think of having a son, I loved the idea of little girls in my life. I couldn't wait to get them moved out to the Detroit area so we could start our new life together. Lillian's family helped take care of her and the girls while I returned to my job in Detroit.

Lillian and I found a cute place in Dearborn, Michigan. Dearborn, the home of Ford Motor Company, was a nice community, and they had a very good local community college so my studies could be picked up again. We made ourselves pretty comfortable as a family and Lillian seemed to be getting excited about the adventure of living in a new area and making new friends. My work kept me extremely busy, including travels to various locations in a five state area for customer meetings and sales training. It was getting to the point where I was gone much of the week traveling to our various branch offices, working with sales people and with customers. Western Union was in the middle of serious change at the time, and competition was kicking in very fast. No more order taking, we would say. It's time to show our customers value and appreciate their business instead of acting like they all owed us something for just showing up. Those days were long gone. Western Union sales people had to learn how to sell.

I was introduced to the martini lunch in Detroit. Bad news for me, but at the time it was what customer's liked to do. Consequently, most of our work had to get done in the morning early. By noon and into the mid afternoon following the 3 hour martini lunches, our day was over, at least we thought. But it was hitting the bars again after we went back to the office smelling like a rotten bottle of booze, then leaving for more meetings at the local bar. Most of the time it was the guys at work talking about getting the job done, and how fucked up everything was at Western Union. I found myself coming home late most evenings half in the bag. Not cool at all. Lillian and I started fighting more and becoming more distant. I wanted her to get involved more in the community, but then she started to withdraw and didn't feel very happy or that she belonged. Lillian was starting to miss home very much. I wanted a beautiful wife waiting for me at home every night whenever I decided to be there. I was not modeling good behavior as a husband or father at the time. I had a very "surface" attitude and did not show unconditional love. And to this day I feel ashamed thinking about these times. Lillian did not deserve this kind of treatment, and I pulled her into my crazy world of corporate greed, booze and success, including my own "big secret" of hiding a mental illness, PTSD as we know it today.

We did become close friends with one of my co-workers Dick and his wife, Mar, and would often go out to their farm for weekends to hang out and for some fishing, along with the drinking Dick loved to do with me at his side. Dick loved "a little shooter" and beer chaser. His favorite whiskey was "smooth as silk" the branding name. Lillian loved his wife, Marlene, and I believe they are still close friends to this day. Marlene helped Lillian with the problems and challenges connected with having a husband who was obsessed with career and booze. Dick was a good friend to me as well. We had lots of fun, but often came dangerously close to killing ourselves on the road home following a week on the road. We stopped often for "a little shooter" then drove on. One time we got so drunk that we got lost, and didn't show up at his house until early in the morning. I remember Lillian standing outside looking so worried and relieved at the same time. She put up with a lot of shit from me. Lillian was a wonderful woman and mother, but I never took the time to appreciate anything other than work at the time and my own selfish needs.

One day a call came in at work from the Area Vice President in Seattle, Washington. He was interested in me joining his team as area sales manager for the 5-state Pacific Northwest Area for Western Union. It took me about 2 seconds to say yes. Getting out of Detroit and back to the west coast after two years in this hell hole was the best news ever. Lillian was excited as well. It didn't take us long to get ready for this move. I sent Lillian and the girl's home to Los Angeles while I flew to Seattle to get on with my new executive responsibilities as area sales manager, working directly under an area vice president with profit and loss responsibilities. At 26-27 years old this was one hell of a break. This was also right at the time in the middle 70's when competition in the telecommunications industry was beginning to take hold. I was just the leader who could capture the imagination of our key customers like Weyerhaeuser Company and Boeing to convince them that Western Union was the right long term partner, especially as the world of data communications was evolving. Telephone companies had the advantage of voice communications, but Western Union was known for its expertise in data communications. Western Union really received praise for installing a Univac computer multi-node store and forward message switching network to bring Telex and TWX together as one, following Western Union's acquisition of TWX. We had also gained significant ground in developing multiplex technology to achieve more bandwidth out of a simple voice grade circuit. Western Union taking the lead again launched the first broadcast satellite, West Star I, putting us into the carrier business to sell wholesale bandwidth to retail telecommunications carriers, government, and large corporations.

While jumping in with both feet and by myself in Seattle, I became too close with one of my co-workers and had an affair. This poor choice changed my whole life and led to a painful divorce with Lillian after 5 years of marriage. It was heart breaking to split up with Lillian and the girls. I hated myself for it, and have not forgiven myself completely after all this time. I still believe that even though we can find excuses for our behavior sometimes like mental health in my case, there is no excuse to hurt others. I hurt Lillian, and broke up our family. Lillian moved back home and had to struggle to get back on her feet as a single mom. Fortunately, she had her loving family to help her, and I continued to provide support in the way of child support for Deanna and Bianca, health benefits, and other ways possible. I had no desire to excuse myself from ongoing responsibilities for my kids, but was relieved to escape from a marriage that was not working. It was and still is painful, but I deserve every moment of pain in my heart after pulling this irresponsible act as a husband and father. I pray to be forgiven and to forgive myself, but it has never come completely. My hope is that my work to make amends will give me peace in the end, along with forgiveness. This is clearly a lifelong challenge and properly so. It goes with accepting responsibility for one's poor choices and for hurting others. I'm a much better man than my behavior at that time would suggest.

To add fuel to the fire, I went on to marry my co-worker Susan after the divorce. This was another very poor choice that I lived with for 9 years. The marriage is considered to this day as a poor choice because Susan worked for the same company, which made the relationship difficult, and Susan was not the right partner for me, nor was I even ready to choose a new partner at the time. It was one great big dumb experience of more pain and hurt that could have been avoided. My anxiety got the best of me so my motivation was finding someone to love that would make all my problems go away. Not so, however, they just got worse.

Susan was threatened by Deanna and Bianca and tried to control my every move to be with them. I let her do it and was not strong enough to fight back. I think Susan tried but she just didn't want to deal with it. As a result, I missed many opportunities to spend quality time with my girls while they were young. I could have had more positive influence on them if I had taken a stronger stand in the beginning. I believe my disposition was weak and broken down at the time, so taking the least path of resistance became the norm.

Western Union started to go through some restructuring during the 1973-74 time periods and my job became at risk. Lots of senior people were fired, including me. The new VP of Marketing did not like me, nor did I like him. Consequently, my 9 year career with Western Union ended. I immediately went to work for Weyerhaeuser Company in Tacoma, Washington, as corporate region telecommunications manager. This would be my chance to get experience as an end user working with service providers to gain a valuable perspective and some technical knowledge on the voice side of the business.

I also had a pretty good relationship with my parents at the time. They seemed to like Susan enough, so did my brother Jerry and his wife Fran. My Dad really started to become mellow in those years and much easier to get along with. Mother and Dad lived in a nice area of Tacoma while Scott, youngest sibling, was finishing HS. Jerry continued not getting along with Dad. It was a constant fight and challenge for Jerry. He would not succeed in trying to reconcile his feelings about the past and could not get anywhere in resolving issues with our parents. They wanted to move on and not dwell on the past. Jerry wanted to get closure and never did.

I left Weyerhaeuser and joined the University of Washington as their first telecommunications manager. This was a fun and challenging job. I had a significant responsibility and budget again along with employees. I also had a great mentor and boss in Ray. I completed my first two years of college in 1975 with an AA degree from South Seattle Community College, and go on to be accepted at the University of Washington, School of Communications. My goal was to continue sharpening my interpersonal communications skills, knowing and also observing over the years how important these skills would be to my ultimate success as a leader. Writing seemed to be a special gift and helped me to a great extent in creating value as an employee. I quickly became known for my writing skills and started to be asked to write for others when important "sales" type proposals needed to be advanced. Selling is required in everything we do whether we want to admit it or not. No one does anything unless there is a value proposition of some kind. You can't assume that if you think it is great that everyone else will too. Selling and getting buy-in from team members is critical in moving your programs and proposals along in the business process.

While at the UW, we were one of the pioneers to prove-in the concept of an adjunct least cost routing and queuing system for using telephone long distance WATS lines more efficiently and cost effectively. These computerized systems would hook on to the main Centrex telephone switching equipment on campus and route all long distance calls. We experienced less than a 12 month payback on savings, and it was guaranteed by the inventor and manufacturer, Action Communications Systems, Dallas, Texas. This is where my relationships in the industry began to grow and lead me back into the sales end of the business later. My reputation for being an innovator became well known in the industry and gave me the "hot commodity" position as a potential employee either on the vendor or end-user side of the business. I also became very active in the Telecommunications Association – Northwest Chapter affording me the opportunity to expand and strengthen my brand. In my mind, it was all about getting results. That's all everyone cared about, results and results now. We had entered a highly competitive new world of information technology with Bill Gates and Microsoft just down the road in Bellevue, Washington, coming up with something that would completely change the world of computing and information technology, a new paradigm was in the making, and it was big, very big.

In the meantime, my own anxiety and disposition worsened. I could never relax and anger would often appear suddenly out of nowhere. I seemed to be pissed off all the time and didn't know why exactly, but now I do. I didn't like myself for much of the time and felt guilty about my success in the business world and failure on the personal side of my life. I really didn't like Susan and wondered why we got married at all. She didn't like anything I liked to do, including outdoor activities, hiking, running in particular, fishing, skiing and all the rest. I loved it as a way to keep me calm about the troublesome feelings I had about my past and how I failed at being a good father and husband. It was critical for me to stay in shape as well. My long standing mental condition continued to be a secret to the extent that I dismissed it at times as nothing more than an early problem in my life. By this time vodka was my main medication. I loved "sneaky Pete's" as I referred to a shot of vodka with a tiny bit of lemon or lime juice. I could knock those out quickly and get high fast without getting sick. I went through vodka just like a Russian, a new quart every other day would work for me. I would discipline myself to stay away from booze during the day by that time. The martini lunch and drinking during the day was long gone by that time as we approached the 1980s when excellence and professionalism all day every day was mandatory to stay fit and competitive to win big. While I was successful to others and to myself on the surface, my internal pain and anxiety was always present. I didn't deserve any of this success!

It didn't take long for me to move on from the University of Washington. Alaska Airlines handed me an offer I couldn't refuse to come in and help them organize a new telecommunications department and set goals to evolve their airline data communications network. I liked the money at Alaska Airlines, and it was a good company. I was able to help them develop new guidelines for managing telecommunications, including a technical support team that functioned more efficiently. They didn't have a fault isolation system in place at the time in the late 70s. Techs would get a call from a remote location in Alaska and immediately jump on an airplane to ride first class to a place like Sitka and fix a problem. The on-site personnel had no procedure to fix a problem without bringing in a technician. As we later learned after launching a new fault isolation procedure that most problems could be easily solved on the spot, or on the phone, or by keeping critical spare parts on hand at each location. Sounds easy enough, but folks at that time and in that environment felt that they could get it done more easily my jumping on the first plane in response to a request. And no kidding, sometimes the computer just needed to be kicked once or twice to get things going again. Agents were not allowed to touch anything. You must assume that the average intelligent person has the capacity to fix most problems when they occur.

I then tried to help Alaska Airlines change out their expensive phone system. I was allowed to do this but my boss at the time did not want his phone, an old six button telephone set (KE6) touched. Otherwise, I could do anything I wanted with the phone system. I had enough of Alaska Airlines after 10 months and couldn't pass up the opportunity to join the Action Communications sales team selling WATSBOX Least Cost Routing systems similar to what we installed at the University of Washington. Besides sitting around in an office drove me crazy and didn't help my anxiety problem at all. Too much time on my hands was not a good thing.

Susan agreed to move down to the Bay Area with me to join my new co-workers at 311 California Street in downtown San Francisco. We bought a home east of Oakland near Walnut Creek. I was ready for a new adventure and this is what the doctor ordered. Susan was able to work for a satellite carrier as well, so it was a good career move for her. There was lots of hope then that our marriage might have a new beginning. I would be much closer to Deanna and Bianca and would have opportunities to travel south to visit them more.

I loved my new job supporting the sales team. Charles and Carl were two of the top sales executives who also worked with me on the University of Washington project. These guys were both nuts and lots of fun. We played hard and worked hard. Working with crazies, and creative ones at that, was the right place for me, a crazy person too. All of us became close friends. Susan worked down the street from me so we were able to get together for lunch often and would travel on Bart to and from work each day. Charles and I remain very close friends to this day, including working together at Nortel Networks and other professional endeavors along the way.

I became much more than a sales support or network engineer because of my sales background. Teaming up on sales calls and for presentations seemed to make us the team to beat. We knocked out competition at every turn, but it was a tough market, everyone fighting for their share of the business.

Susan started drinking more and seemed to be unhappy lots of the time. We were fighting more as time went on. The environment at Action started to change as well, so our office in downtown San Francisco was at risk. We were considered the party bunch from San Francisco, and became suspect by our superiors, and eventually they started a restructuring and closed down the office. By 1981, I left Action and returned to Seattle. For a short time I worked for Interconnect Northwest, a retail telephone equipment provider, later becoming Cascade Telecom. I brought my good friend Carl in to work with me to help steer the company forward. But Carl had other ideas and wanted to run the company. I was eventually fired under some very hurtful conditions. Trust was compromised completely and the residual effect on my disposition was not favorable. Carl and I lost our great friendship for good at that time. I could never trust him again.

During that time Susan's drinking problem, and mine too, became totally out of control. We fought and fought. She drank more and more and had black outs. She even tried to beat me up a couple of times, including kicking me in the groin area. She was driving the Cadillac while I was driving the Pinto. One day, after returning to Action Communications in a new sales executive capacity in the Pacific Northwest, I went down and purchased a new Datsun 240Z. I always wanted a fast car. I purchased the vehicle completely on my own and drove it up to our home at the end of the cul-de-sac in Redondo Beach (Washington) and honked the horn. Susan came out and yelled at me and said I was not allowed to purchase the car without her permission. I gave her the finger drove off. Our marriage ended not long after this incident after nine years of a highly questionable marriage. There was no real love. Hell, I still didn't know what love was all about, but would soon learn. To this day the only regret is getting married to her in the first place, and the sadness and hurt this experience brought to Lillian and the breaking up of our family. It was done but not without pain and more anxiety on top of anxiety that did not help my mental condition, still a well kept big secret. I will acknowledge, however, that Susan's parents remain a very fond memory of that time. Her father Herbert and mother Myrtle were dear people who are now gone. I never returned to visit them and wished I had. Her Dad was heard saying one time that he thought his daughter ruined our marriage with her drinking. Well, that may have contributed to our problems, but it took two of us.

My loving wife and soul mate Judy and I have been married now for 27 years on April 21, 2011. We knew each other as friends in the telecommunications industry long before we were married. We did become close at the end of my marriage to Susan. Judy has given me more joy in life and peace than anything I have ever experienced. I know now what unconditional love is all about. I didn't experience true love until later in life, but glad it finally came. Judy is loved by my children Deanna and Bianca and grandchildren, Joey, Jordan, Mike, and Cameryn. Judy and I met our daughter Sarah when she was just a few hours old. We were chosen by her birth parents, which is very special. Sarah is now 23 and in her last year of college at the University of Oregon. I've been blessed at this point in my life, and the "big secret" finally came clean while doing research on my Dad's war years and the symptoms of PTSD, including how it affects family members as a legacy of war. I don't have to keep a secret anymore after all these years. It is a true feeling of freedom, and the beginning of a new period of healing. I can now go on with the rest of my life doing the things that bring me joy, loving Judy and my family, and finally feeling peace in my heart. The old throb in my chest is now gone. I do continue to treat my PTSD symptoms, but with an open mind and no shame.

My career continued on with Nortel Networks for many years, eventually being promoted to the position of vice president of sales, along with being honored with the highest achievement of recognition, "Masters." My burning desire to succeed and strong leadership qualities worked well into the later years of my career with many successes along the way. I finally earned my BA in Management at St. Mary's College in Moraga, California. I owe much to Nortel for giving me the chance to pursue a wonderful career and for funding my college education. My college graduation was a special time in 1990, when my father Vernon, daughters Bianca and little Sarah, Brother Scott, wife Judy, and other friends joined me in recognizing an accomplishment that took about 20 years to complete. It is still one of the most proud moments of my life and the one accomplishment in terms of my education that will always be treasured.

Judy by my side, we eventually relocated to Leavenworth, Washington, to pursue a new life in the mountains and to raise Sarah in a small town. Judy pursued her new career in early childhood special education, while I returned to my career at various times and did mostly management consulting work. We even owned a small retail business in Leavenworth for a few years, which was clearly a character building experience. I became very active in highly rewarding community service while living in Leavenworth, including volunteer and teaching roles in education at the local high school and community college. Education is the highest priority to me and represents a critical success factor for our children's future. Everything I have learned and experienced points right back to education. The more educated we are the more intelligent choices we make as individuals, as families, as friends, and as Americans.

I stopped drinking alcohol in Leavenworth some 11 years ago. The decision to put alcohol in my past changed everything for the better as well. It also helped my marriage become much stronger and a more loving experience. Judy and I are the best of friends and have fun together. Sure we have a struggle or two at times and few challenges, but all in all it is the best life can offer.

We retired, so we say, to Depoe Bay, Oregon, six years ago after living in Leavenworth for 15 years. Judy still works part time helping birth to toddler children with special needs. I now devote all my time to helping kids with a wonderful non-profit as board member of www.neighborsforkids.org. I'm doing the best work of my life, and not even getting paid for it. It's a way to give back and to support kids who need mentoring and a better chance at life with help in improving their education and getting prepared to be responsible and contributing members of society. As a board member I can also offer my strong business, marketing, and leadership qualities to this organization at a critical time. I'll no doubt spend the rest of my time devoted to this kind of social cause, making a difference each day of my remaining years.

PART II

LIVING AND COPING WITH PTSD

Living with a Family Member Diagnosed with PTSD

The author is not a mental health professional! My story represents the human behaviors observed in my own family resulting from living with my Dad, who was diagnosed right after WWII with "Battle Fatigue" now known as Post Traumatic Stress Disorder (PTSD). My goal at this point in writing the story is to share my experience with those who are challenged with similar symptoms resulting from living in a toxic home culture, especially those that live with returning veterans who suffer with PTSD, including WWII, Vietnam, Iraq, & Afghanistan. The inter-generational transfer of PTSD symptoms is of huge importance since we need to break the cycle of abuse and life-long effects on families. The questions we need to ask ourselves now are what have we learned, and what can we do differently. With my own life experience, along with many others, what can we take away and give to those who have needed help for many years and those that are just beginning to experience life with a returning veteran or anyone who has suffered a traumatic experience?

Your loved ones sometimes come home a different person than they were when they left for combat duty. What can you do now to help them transition back to living a full and productive life? What can you and other family members do to give them comfort and relief from the terrible anxiety and fears they are living with? How do we become paraprofessionals in the mental health business? We have to change, and change is hard. We need more education. We need more coping skills. We need to find patience and love. We need to use outside resources more effectively. We need to recognize symptoms and treat symptoms. War is our legacy too. We "served" as family members. Now it is your turn to fight, a fight that will return your loved one to the person you once knew or to coach them to manage their lives differently and to make adjustments. They put their life at risk and survived; the least we can do is to give them the strength to live on. More importantly, as a loving family member or friend, your commitment and effort could

90

save your life and prevent you from acquiring the same symptoms of PTSD, making this tragedy an intergenerational challenge.

It would have been wonderful if my Father, Vernon, and Mother, Marcella were provided some miracle treatment in their time to cope with the disturbing symptoms of PTSD and the effects on loved ones living with them, their children. We can dream all we want, but the reality is that there was nothing at the time except experimentation with alcohol and/ or finding ways individually to cope. Even then not knowing the extent of the condition nor understanding the symptoms, including the stigma placed on mental health issues, provided my parents with much to work with. Consequently, we must look forward and look at the lessons learned from analyzing the experience of family members and others to seek out solutions over time. My goal with myself and my family is to break the cycle. We have to start somewhere. And right now is not soon enough from my perspective.

On the ideal side, and to dream a bit about how it could have been when Dad first came home from WWII and was diagnosed with "battle fatigue", the following describes what is now available to returning soldiers from battle. This is an example of technology at its best and how it may have changed everything if it had been available during the early years following WWII.

PTSD and Anxiety Treatment Helps Soldiers Returning Home from War

Alpha-Stim cranial electrotherapy stimulation is a technology cleared by the FDA and the DOD/VA for use as sole or complementary treatment for anxiety, insomnia, PTSD and more. The technology is showing promise with soldiers returning home from war with tons of information at Alpha-Stim.com.

Mineral Wells, TX, March 31, 2011--(PR.com)-- 3 out of 4 veterans are now choosing a new technology for the treatment of anxiety, mood disorder, stress and PTSD. Alpha-Stim technology by Electro-medical Products International, Inc. is a pocket-sized device with electrodes emitting from it that go onto the ear by the way of ear clips. A low level current in a precise wave form is then delivered into the brain for twenty to sixty minute sessions at a time.

The technology is cleared by the FDA and the DOD/VA as a standalone or complementary treatment for a variety of ailments. The costs of the treatment are minimal and each Alpha-Stim device comes with a five year warranty. According to Daniel L. Kirsch, PhD, Chairman of Electromedical Products International, the company that designed the Alpha-Stim technology, side effects are rare, minor and self-limiting. The side effects the doctor mentions include headaches and skin reactions at the electrode sites.

Recently, Alpha-Stim technology has shown promise with members of the armed forces. In 2005, Alpha-Stim was included in the Federal Supply Schedule for the DOD/VA and the US Army is currently using Alpha-Stim technology in the treatment of post traumatic stress disorder and for chronic pain. In fact, according to the manufacturer, more than 63 Veterans Affairs Medical Centers have ordered the devices for the treatment of various ailments and 3 out of 4 veterans choose the technology for their treatment over 4 other choices in a VA study.

Sounds like low level electro-shock treatment to me, but certainly shows what we can do right now. It hurts me to think of the huge value this sort of technology may have had 60 years ago, and even 40 years ago when I was diagnosed with "emotional instability" in the U.S. Navy.

There is little or no value in focusing on "what could have been" or sitting around whining and feeling sorry for ourselves. But it is informative and encouraging to know that we have come very far in understanding, diagnosing and treating PTSD symptoms. What we need to do now is to try and help the tens of thousands of people who suffer from symptoms from an inter-generational PTSD standpoint and from other more subtle ways of developing the symptoms. Awareness is the first big step in healing all of us who have had to live in an experimental and sometimes dangerous and risky world of little or no understanding of what is happening or has happened to us.

Coping with PTSD Symptoms in the Real World

I found ways to cope with my less than understood PTSD symptoms, but did not know what was driving my obsession with achievement through work and education. I never got to the root problem until now. I'm not sure if changing a thing would have made it better, or finding out the root problem earlier would have done anything incrementally different. It could have possibly had an adverse affect in the context of creating an "excuse" mindset, leading me more toward flight vs. fight in terms of self development and career. On the personal side, my experience strongly suggests flight, since running away from my problems at times has been apparent throughout my life. As age provided more experience and wisdom, "running away" became less apparent. I started making big attempts to solve personal problems, especially in my marriage to Judy. I stopped drinking alcohol 11 years ago as a big step in the right direction, and consequently saved my marriage.

Rather than continuing to be confused about the subject of coping with symptoms in experimental ways, let's review the broadly accepted symptoms of Post Traumatic Stress Disorder (PTSD). Reviewing the symptoms and connecting my own experiences as well as other members of my family, including possibly other subjects, will help us to manage the symptoms more effectively at a personal treatment level before even entering into professional therapy. The intent of this very practical approach is to encourage people suffering with these symptoms to be less fearful of professional treatment and to start healing wounds as quickly as possible. I waited too long. Many years of pain could have been mitigated and managed more effectively if I had been educated much earlier or had not been in denial.

"It's dumbfounding to understand just how much damage can be done by one human being. One thing I try to remember about humans is this: one person can change history by a negative choice and one person change history with a good choice. Choosing to heal is a good choice. It helps change life for you now and in the future. It prevents unnecessary pain for yourself and others. It heals you, it helps heal others. Your choice to reach out is a good choice as well and it matters."

I took the above quote from an article, "What are Your Hyper Vigilance and Hyper Arousal Symptoms?" published by Sun Drip Journals. It clearly reinforces my desire and that of others to reach out, share, and heal from traumatic events that result in suffering from the symptoms of PTSD. So far my knowledge of the subject is exponentially larger than before, and knowing more about my past and current behaviors allows a form of treatment for healing and to mitigate certain behaviors that are actually over the top. My intensity works well in a sales type environment where my career flourished over the years. But working with a board in a non-profit and social services culture is not conducive to excessive intensity caused by hyper vigilance & hyper arousal. You simply push people away and make them nervous or resentful or they feel threatened. This has been a career long behavior of my experience, working very well and effectively in a competitive highly intense and sense of urgency culture, that being sales & marketing. But it can be troublesome and potentially destructive behavior in a less intense world of people focused on a kinder and gentler daily lifestyle. And on a personal level, my wife of 27 years has helped me to become more tolerant of others who are less intense because that is who she is or who they are. It's helped me to diffuse the "over the top" intensity referred to and shows how important it is to have a support system that can tolerate and coach a person suffering from PTSD symptoms, specifically those referred to here.

Some of the signs of PTSD usually include several of the following symptoms:

- Re-occurring or sustained depression. An evaluation of the symptoms of depression can be provided by most doctors.
- Anxiety or panic attacks
- Flashbacks or re-occurring nightmares.
- Emotional "numbing"
- Hyper-vigilance
- Alienation, tendency to isolate or social distancing
- Loss of memory and concentration
- Alcohol or drug dependence (usually to numb the emotional pain)
- Inability to form intimate or trusting relationships.
- Recurring anger or rage
- Suicidal thoughts or obsession
- A prolonged feeling of "fore-shortening" This is the troubling thoughts that your life will be cut short in the near future.
- Startle response

Evolution of PTSD

Post Traumatic Stress Disorder (PTSD) is not new research or discovery. In 1993, the Dept of Veterans Affairs raised questions about mental health issues in previous wars. A study was initiated using records from doctors who had participated in wars as far back as the Civil War.

The list of syndromes and disorders include,

- U.S. Civil War – Irritable Heart and Nostalgia
- WWI – Effort syndrome/Soldier's Heart and Shell Shock
- WWII/Korea – Effort syndrome and Battle Fatigue/Combat Exhaustion (acute combat stress reaction)
- Vietnam War – Agent Orange Exposure and Post Vietnam syndrome (PTSD)
- Gulf War – Gulf War syndrome and adjustment reaction/PTSD

The study showed that in all these cases of varied psychiatric illnesses persisted following each war and often during the wars with PTSD representing the larger umbrella of symptoms discussed in this story. All of the syndromes shared common symptoms, including fatigue, shortness of breath, headache, sleep disturbances, forgetfulness, and difficulty concentrating. There is also a long history of government concern for veterans who experienced unexplained symptoms. And there has been an effort by the government to create specialized health care centers, conduct research, and compensate veterans. It was also reported in cases of Israeli soldiers that there were similar psychological problems among family members, an initial indication of the inter-generational impact of PTSD, the subject of this story. Follow-up studies were also conducted using British military health records showing similar symptom clusters.

It was only after Vietnam that the government launched more aggressive research and defined all these syndromes and symptoms into one category, PTSD. The majority of veterans in most previous wars starting with Vietnam ended up returning home without adequate diagnosis and treatment, leaving our combat soldiers to experiment on their own, which often led to a toxic culture at home and subsequent trauma experienced by family members.

Perpetual Anxiety

Does using the word "perpetual" in the context of anxiety sound painful? I can hardly remember moments in my adult life in particular without anxiety. It is a throbbing pit in one's stomach that never goes away. It hurts and seems to take hold as if it had its own life.

Once freedom from my toxic home life was realized upon joining the Navy in 1963, a new phase of anxiety emerged. It was initially very scary to be on my own, to build my life without the constant feeling of being trapped or imprisoned in a dysfunctional existence. Now, I had to prove myself and really never had the opportunity to do so before entering the U.S. Navy. The new type of anxiety was different, however, but still troublesome. The new fuel for my anxiety was success in being the best at everything presented to me. I set high goals and expectations of myself, sometimes not very realistic. I didn't leave much margin for error, and hated to put myself in a position to get criticism, even if it was constructive. I wanted to get it right the first time and really didn't accept constructive criticism at that time. "Coaching" as I know it well today, was considered in the same way as my parents pounding on me with statements regarding my inability to succeed or being less as a person than others. Somehow, I learned how to play the game with myself but at a high expense as it turned out.

When there is a lack of balance and one is not grounded in positive ways in the first place, it is not possible to win peace of mind or to mitigate anxiety because other important ingredients are missing such as trust, love, and respect for self and others. I had to learn late in life how to trust and love others, including myself.

In my toxic home culture, survival was the name of the game. It was like being in a foxhole all the time, or as my Dad would say sometimes, "it was battle stations practically all the time" when he was at sea fighting in the Asiatic Pacific Theater. Consequently, one could conclude that inter-generational PTSD could be acquired through simulation of a "battle stations" condition at home as a child. We were in a constant state of fear, anxious about when Dad would go off, or when Mother would freak out. A normal position at home when Dad walked by was defensive in terms of putting arms and hands over heads for protection of a potential blow that might come out of nowhere. My brothers and I had to be ready for anything all the time, morning, noon, or night. Moments of tranquility came when we were alone in the house when the parents were not there.

As a young sailor going to boot camp it was highly structured and I knew what to expect. It really wasn't too bad. I even manipulated my way into the head detail, Master-at-Arms, to avoid doing some of the morning exercises that were tough since my physical condition was not good on the left side from polio. I had a weak left arm and left chest with muscles that didn't develop into equal strength like my right side. Doing push-ups was especially difficult or lifting weights. Last thing I needed was for the drilling instructor to discover some weakness and disqualify me from the Navy and send me home. This would have been a disaster. I needed to get through boot camp to save my life. I made it through boot camp with flying colors. What a glorious day in my new life as an adult! My first real success as a man came. I could succeed in doing something really important and make a difference. I loved the camaraderie as well. I loved the competitive and fair environment where we were all equal and treated like human beings. The Navy started out as the best place for me at the time. It opened up my world as an adult. I could set goals and prove something to myself and others.

During boot camp there were many tests to determine what skill set potential we had that we didn't know about. The Navy was good at that. I tested very high on the radio and electronics testing for some reason. Never thought this would be my future but quickly realized it opened the door to getting orders to radio school in San Diego, California. I did so poorly in high school with a D average, it was a wonder I could even get into the Navy at 17 without a HS diploma in the first place. But from a vocational skills standpoint it appeared that my career might fit nicely into a place in radio communications as a Radioman. This title went well with the last name of Sparks since this is what they called radiomen in the Navy anyway. I figured it was fate at work at the time.

Radio school was a blast as well. I continued to do well with my studies and graduated in the top 10% of my class. I went home a few times looking for pats on the back from family members and love but quickly turned to relationships with girls that were not the best. It was difficult to build relationships with the opposite sex for me in the beginning. I didn't have very much confidence in myself and was highly insecure. I felt better hanging out with the guys and going down to Tijuana at times and getting drunk and finding love in this rotten place. I paid for my fun in Mexico by contracting a good case of an STD requiring treatment and confinement for a time while going to school. I even scared myself half to death because I did have a girl friend up north in the San Pedro area I was seeing for a time. There wasn't sex in the mix to the extent that I could pass this on to her, but I really didn't know. So, it was consequently the right thing for me to tell her and get her tested. That relationship ended on the spot after her parents found out about her dating a sailor that picked up an STD. Not a good thing at the time, believe me. This little mishap made me feel more insecure, embarrassed and withdrawn, so back to my studies in radio school and enough of trying to have a life larger than what was structured and manageable. I didn't need to get myself in trouble and kicked out of the Navy to be sure.

Following graduation from Radioman School my orders came for Comsubflot-5 Naval Submarine Communications Command in Pearl Harbor, Hawaii. How could a dumb surfer from Southern California get shore duty orders in Hawaii? I thought I had died and gone to heaven. I was on my way to paradise and the best surf in the world, not to mention hanging out at the beach with beautiful girls. My new life was really looking like a winner at this point. I believe my Dad even felt proud of me at the time. And this was something that I needed very much in my life.

Returning to my earlier story, my emotional challenges began to emerge after being in Hawaii for awhile, working, meeting new friends, and getting into healthy relationships for a time. I needed a close relationship, however, and this is when I fell in love big time with Sheryl and almost got married. My life in paradise quickly turned from a good thing to a troublesome life challenge that included being diagnosed with "emotional instability," effectively ending my career in the U. S. Navy after two years.

The big challenges of coping with symptoms related to PTSD really started to kick-in. My coping strategy was all about denial and staying totally busy with work, succeeding and going to school. This was my way of managing the constant knot in my stomach caused by worry and anxiety that failure was just around the corner. Feeling alone and without mentoring or a caring family made it very difficult to navigate during my free time and in getting more than 4 hours of restful sleep at night. I awakened consistently with nightmares and sweating. At that time the only medication was alcohol during brief free time and hard work and study during my responsible hours of the day. I hated to not have anything to keep me occupied all the time. This treatment strategy was so critical that being married did not offer the balance that could free me from the persistent knot in my stomach. I was not able to know or experience unconditional love to the extent that it offered security and self confidence that was needed and would come later in life. Even having children did not provide me with the feeling of self worth and making a difference in the lives of my kids. What in the hell was I searching for and couldn't seem to find? We'll find out later. In the meantime, I started to turn into an angry person, one of the other symptoms of PTSD.

Promotion to Radioman Third Class while stationed at Comsubflot-5

Self-Destructive Behavior

"Clinical reports suggest that many adults who engage in self-destructive behavior have childhood histories of trauma and disrupted parental care. The nature of the trauma and the subjects' age at the time of the trauma affected the character and the severity of the self-destructive behavior." (http://ajp.psychiatryonline.org/cgi/content/abstract/148/12/1665)

Scott Sparks, United States Air Force 1983

My Little Bro Scotty's "Crash & Burn" Story

After much research, especially with respect to my own family and our toxic world as children, there is a clear thread of various levels of self-destructive behavior both in personal and professional experiences. My youngest brother, Scotty, wrote to me with his own experience as a child and some of his traumatic episodes, which contributed to his own self-destructive behavior in his professional life. Scotty recalls he was 9 years old when his childhood ended. His older brothers were long gone, and sister, Laura, was about to leave home following a very traumatic period of abuse and a tragic personal event. Scotty was very close to his sister, who he was able to grow up with since the difference in age was relatively close, 8 years apart. I was horrified and emotional reading about my younger brother's experience. I'll try to relate some it here in appropriate context, but keep most of it confidential as he requested.

In Scotty's words, "At 9 years old I liked to play a game with aluminum foil and wooden garden stakes; I would mold the foil to my face and body, creating a suit of armor and fashion swords out of the stakes. Mother and Dad's friends were visiting that day. Loretta, a close friend, asked me to meet her in my room; she had something I needed to know. As we sat down together in my room, I was told the "bad news" about my big sister, Laura. As the story goes on, I can't remember how much later it was (maybe a few months), Mother was hospitalized for surgery (I also think this was somewhere around the time you and first wife, Lillian and the kids moved to Washington and stayed with us for awhile). Anyway, that time was such a blur to me; there was so much fighting in the home and amongst family members; it was hard to keep track of who was friend or foe. Everyday seemed like another drama, with the biggest drama between Laura and Dad. While Mother was in the hospital they "spit nails" at each other daily, which culminated in a neighborhood scene: Dad, wearing only his underwear chasing after Laura and her car, in the middle of the street.

This is when my academics starting to go south; missing lots of school days (neither parent connected this to what was happening at home). I also started sneaking drinks of wine from Mother's gallon jugs she kept in the fridge, along with an occasional valium (Dad kept a full jar in his closet). Finally, the lack of sleep from "all-nighter" fights between family members became intolerable. All of this makes me tired now, many years later, just to recall those times.

The biggest blow to me came the following summer. I was playing in our garage, walking on the stilts that Laura had made for me, I was happy that it was summer and was looking forward to my 10th birthday. Laura came out to the garage, called me over and gave me a big hug. Then she stood me in front of her and told me she was leaving to live in California. I tried to be a "big boy" about it and remember holding back tears in her presence; but as soon as she left the garage I remember sitting on the garage floor crying uncontrollably. After she left I had nightmares that she was dead and I saw her in her coffin.....I missed my sister terribly and to tell the truth I still miss her today.

After Laura left Mother was devastated, her normal bouts of complaining intensified to more frequent and longer in duration and Dad became less tolerant; frequent argument and fights continued as well as conflicts with extended family. I continued to do poorly in school, and battled with drug and alcohol use until the 11th grade, which for a period up to my fourth year in the service, was not an issue. Following all this heavy alcohol use and severe bouts of depression, including anxiety, all have been an intermittent part of my life, as well as many of the other symptoms you describe in your book, *Reconciliation, a Son's Story*.

Although it was very emotional writing to you with this tale of woe, writing it down and sharing with you has given me some healing effect. I want to write more, but need to take a break and get myself back together again."

Sadly, Scotty's story demonstrates how long term abuse or trauma in the case of a child becomes a life-time PTSD issue. I had no idea that my little brother, Scotty, experienced this kind of pain as a child. It causes me to regret not taking the time to understand better the circumstances or our own family's toxic culture. Too many times, I have made assumptions and jumped to conclusions about certain behaviors of my siblings, only to take the low road of a less educated and compassionate person.

Growing up as a "2ⁿᵈ Class Citizen"

Feeling socially distanced and alienated was normal. The PTSD symptoms of social distancing and alienation reminded me of growing up with parents who really believed they couldn't be the best and have the best. We were a 2ⁿᵈ class family! I know my dad should have felt great and wanted to be great. I believe his emotional circumstances caused by "battle fatigue" during WWII made him feel down even more so. I can also see clearly that my mother, growing up during the Depression era, felt she was from a less than deserving social standing. I'm not convinced looking back that military families in the "white hat" category held a position of high esteem during the 50s following WWII and Korean War. All of this started to change, although slowly, during the time I joined the Navy in 1963. Living this life both as a "military brat" and as sailor in the Navy during all those years provides me with the ability to compare and contrast. All men and women in all branches of the modern military serve with distinction and return home as heroes whether they were injured or sadly killed in combat or not. Local responders stand right behind our military as community service heroes as well. We have come a long way in giving our military and local emergency service community the respect they always deserved. *"Thank you for your service"* is now part of our American culture.

As the son of a highly decorated Navy combat veteran, and a student of what it takes to be successful, along with a huge ego, I was not about to allow the "2nd class citizen" baggage to follow me in my own life journey. Virtually everything I pursued on a professional level was my best work. I just kept getting better and better and better. Perfection and total success was the only path for me. Sadly, this passion and drive adversely affected my personal life and prevented me until around age 36-37 from building a balance so that loving relationships could be realistic and extremely beneficial. This is where PTSD served me well for the most part; my professional life and pursuits, along with the relationships that went with being a top professional in the IT industry. I love statements like *"failure is not an option."* My professional record speaks for itself in the most positive ways, but my personal life for the first half was not much to write home about. I have now become much closer to being the person I intended to be on the personal side. I work on it still everyday with much help from my loving wife, Judy. I also know well who gets apologies from me, and sometimes more than once. I do this directly and indirectly to make sure these good and loving people know that my apology is sincere and from the heart.

"Laugh Your Ass Off"- Coping with Anxiety

The best therapy for coping with PTSD symptoms, especially anxiety, is laughing and laughing and more laughing. I walked into this type of therapy solution quite by accident by testing the waters early on in my career saying and doing stupid things, and being obnoxious. Of course, timing is everything. This is one of those things you see on TV that we are told not to try at home or it could be a disaster. And it was a disaster for me at times. But most of the time it worked, and it is still fun with my best friends even today.

The first time this really took hold and got my attention is when one of my bosses, Joe, Area Sales Manager, Western Union, Detroit, Michigan, walked into my office one day and raised up his leg and farted, big time! This happened around 1970 while I was being introduced to my new job as city sales manager for Western Union in Detroit. This was my first promotion to a serious management position, so my anxiety was at a high level. I really couldn't understand why they sent me all the way to Detroit from Los Angeles as a 22-23 year old kid to take on this big responsibility to turn-around a sales team that was sitting on its hands for the most part.

So, old Joe broke the ice with a loud and thunderous fart. My creative talents helped me calculate immediately that this was a modeling behavior by a good leader that would help me with my own style, and to help me relax and be calm. And it really does work, especially if you are working in a highly stressful sales culture or any type of creative environment where people are generally goofy anyway. Don't do this around serious accountants or boring office managers, or folks who do everything by the book. Being nuts on the job is usually not studied nor recommended in school either.

From then on it was "stupid is, as stupid does", but it was carefully choreographed by me and my good friends and co-workers who would go along with me on this journey. And I'm talking about really intelligent, educated, and successful people behaving in a childlike manner at the appropriate time. I can't think of anything better than taking every opportunity to laugh and laugh often.

I'll never forget another example when working for Action Communications Systems in the late 70s and early 80s. The entire national sales team traveled to Dallas, Texas for an important sales meeting with the CEO of the company. We were all in deep shit because our numbers were not good at the time, so we all thought our days were numbered anyway, so we had nothing to lose.

During the CEO's talk to us at the sales meeting held at our favorite hotel, HOJO's (Howard Johnsons) in Plano, Texas, most of the sales team became restless and anxious during the meeting. It had been 3 days into the meeting, so we were close to going home and couldn't wait to get the hell out of there either back on the job or looking for a new job. We couldn't stand anymore bullshit from the executive team, including the CEO. We were all down and dirty high tech sales people who did well outside of the office selling but hated every second sitting around in a crowded sales meeting listening to people who pretended to be inspirational and motivating. We already knew what was happening in the market place and didn't need these pretentious fools telling us what we already knew. Action had a corner on the least cost routing (LCR) market until then, and now had competition. The easy sale was in our past. We had to get better at showing value and proving our case to customers who bought our products too easily in the past. All we had to do is show up most of the time and get them to sign the order. Now, we had several hot shots showing up before and after our sales calls and building a story that sounded a whole lot better than the Action Communication's ho-hum presentation.

As our CEO was talking, we intentionally started to be distracting. One guy started popping popcorn in the back of the conference room. Others kept talking and laughing among themselves and would not listen. One sales guy had a bag of medications or pills he would be running back to the restroom and popping all afternoon. We couldn't believe this guy was so bold. My bet, considering the timing around the late 70s, snorting coke was a pastime during the sales meeting as well. Around that time cocaine was just starting to get attention and was legal for awhile, but considered a naughty thing to do. To this day, it is hard to believe that this CEO at the time would take all this disrespect from the sales team, but he did, and left the meeting. We won, at least temporarily. The VP of Sales & Marketing, Mike, kicked our asses and restricted us to the hotel for the rest of the time we were there. He even made us work into the evening. Mike was tough but that is the kind of leadership we needed at the time. Mike was a big guy, and he spanked us pretty good and we deserved it. It was also one of the best laughing experiences we ever had, and we kept the story alive for years and still do today when some of us get together. The CEO was also replaced shortly after that sales meeting.

Once returning to our offices in the field, with new sales collaterals and value propositions to fight the battle, we launched into an attack on competition, and got back on track with a strong performance. We always pulled through no matter what happened. We were a team, like brothers in battle fighting a war. We stuck together, drank together, laughed together, smoked dope and snorted coke together, but got the job done. That was the late 70s and early 80s, but political correctness started to kick-in during the mid 80s and we had to tone down a bit then.

It was a big shock to me, as a professional and on the conservative side, to observe that our office in San Francisco appeared to be a front for dealing drugs most of the time back then in the late 70s. I would walk into the office and often bump into three-piece suited guys and gals running in and out. Some were snorting coke, and others were weighing and bagging marijuana in the back-office. But we laughed, and laughed, and got the job done. I really didn't like it but had to go with the flow without becoming judgmental with my peers. We somehow survived this chaotic period of transitioning to competition in the telecom industry, which in the past was completely owned by the phone companies. The monopoly was disappearing overnight and we were adjusting to it. The anxiety was high, even higher for me with my PTSD symptoms, not understood at the time. I thought at times I was going crazy, but did make it through this period and go on to bigger and better career pursuits along with failed marriages. It was a welcome sign to me when the office antics started changing and demanded that we behave in a more professional manner. Big adjustments had to be made for us to continue our careers in a hot information technology industry where lots of money could be made. We had to find other ways to manage anxiety, leaving the free-wheeling less than disciplined work ethic in our past. We continued to find ways to laugh, however, but more discretely and at the right times and places.

My most favorite laughing partners included Charles and Jim. I worked with both and became close friends for many years. Jim passed away at 58, entirely too young, of course. I don't believe any of us knew he had a heart condition. Jim was always fit and modeled excellent leadership and professionalism. But Jim loved to laugh, and we found our ways before and after sales calls or sales meetings to get the laughing done. Jim was an example of the best mix of personal and professional qualities for me to thrive in my work. He allowed me to be myself, but at the same time demanded professionalism and results.

My best friend Charles and I have known each other now going on 40 years. We have worked together at different companies, including Nortel Networks, and have remained close friends for all this time. When Charles and I get together in person or on the phone it is like going to a Las Vegas comedy relief show. Charles finally retired in the summer of 2011. He is one of the few of us who were able to survive well into his 60's in a tough

IT business. His demeanor was always in his favor; calm, cool, collected, and really funny. Charles was always the guy you wanted on your team. He knew how to get results and customers loved him. We transitioned through many good times and challenges together and laughing always helped us through the tough times. I needed it more than Charles and he somehow knew that, and went along with me as I instigated opportunities to be goofy and to laugh together until our guts hurt.

I place a very high value on a hand full of friends in my life, including my own wife, Judy. Charles, Jim and Les are three of my closest friends. Charles showed me how to laugh and keep laughing. Although Jim passed away too early in his life at age 58, he remains in my heart as one of my dearest friends. Les and I have been close friends since the early 80s when I first joined Nortel Networks. Les has always modeled friendship consistent with his spiritual beliefs and in unconditional ways. In retirement, Byron, one of my neighbors, has become a very close friend. We have become best friends and good partners in our community service endeavors. I can always go back to trust and respect as the key factors in lasting friendships. My intense behavior and anxiety does represent a challenge for maintaining long and close friendships. Knowing more about my condition now makes me appreciate even more all those friends who put up with me for so many years. If I had known more about my condition earlier it would have been easier to manage friendships better. But for the most part there are very special memories that resulted from friends who had that extra patience with me and saw something that was genuine, someone they could count on and trust. And for me it was the same with all of these very close and dear friends, Charles, Jim, Les and Byron. And there are others as well who made an impact on my life. Although Jim is gone, I do miss him very much and think about him most days. He seems to be there reminding me of things that make a difference in my behavior and in the treatment of others.

Is Anger Channeling an Inherent Response?

The answer is probably yes and no. It appears to be a self defense mechanism looking at the experiences of my family members and others. If I had known earlier, that anger is a serious symptomatic condition that should be treated and mitigated sooner than later I may have done some things differently. But not so fast, I was angry for many years and it was painful feeling this way. It took at least 30 or more years for me not to be angry anymore. Anger worked when it was focused on professional endeavors that required the extra testosterone and aggressiveness required in my line of work, sales and marketing, and in turning around failing or failed business plans. They called me "Mr. Fix it" or AKA "hatchet man." Those people suffering from PTSD symptoms like to be in control. You also have to be brutal and less than caring about others, especially those who are targets for termination or performance improvement. I developed some armor protecting myself from feelings of compassion so that I could carry out my orders to turn-around the business relationship with customers.

Happy customers were my reward and security. I focused completely on building excellent customer relationships and talented team members who were behind me in getting things done in quick and sometimes messy ways. I was never in one job or assignment for more than two years. I loved being sent in when everything and everybody, including customers were in complete chaos and pissed off at my company. I worked well during an emergency or crisis or when no one else seemed to know what to do. I could get away with throwing my weight around, firing people, hiring people, and fighting with people. This kind of work empowered me, and made me feel secure, but only in a temporary way. I needed to go on to the next fight when one fight was finished, either getting promoted or sometimes fired. Customers loved me. Employees who made lots of money loved me. Most were a tad afraid and threatened with my aggressive and intense style. It was excellent treatment for one of the worst symptoms of PTSD, anger.

But when anger joined me at home or on a personal level it didn't work so well, not well at all in fact. I was never physical, but my voice was loud and scary. I would call it mental or emotional abuse, another symptom of a person suffering from PTSD. I thank God to this day that I am not and never have been a person who was compelled to use physical means or force on others, especially women. I have always respected women in my life, especially on a professional level. Women were front and center with the good stuff needed to help balance my aggressive behavior. Women have compassion for the most part and were gentle but still effective in their dealings with others. I thought highly of this attribute and quality in women professionals as compared to my male counterparts who rarely measured up for the most part. Think what you will on this scenario, but it was a way for me to find the balance needed to get my work done effectively without getting myself into big trouble from an HR standpoint.

Age has worked miracles for me in terms of becoming a kinder and gentler person. Working in a social services non-profit culture, and living with a kind and compassionate partner for close to 30 years has made me a different person all together. And I like myself these days as I approach age 65.

Adding my own experience to the mix, there appears to be a consistent thread in my family's case in channeling anger in positive or at least constructive ways rather than being destructive to others or self-destructive. My Dad, Vernon, as an example, continued his career following the U.S. Navy with the Federal Bureau of Prisons as mentioned earlier in this story. Dad could go to work in this environment and kick around in-mates who acted out, and he acted as though it was a pleasure. He talked about it and bragged all the time about using his position to "straighten out" these incarcerated prisoners. He was also a drug abuse counselor, of all things. He didn't drink alcohol anymore so had gotten his substance abuse problem resolved during most of his career in the Bureau of Prisons. He seemed to be on the calmer side of his past angry disposition as he progressed in the Federal Bureau of Prisons. It would be appropriate to conclude then that he was able to release much of his angry tendencies through his work, which could be considered constructive. Dad was responsible for the brig while aboard ship in the Navy as well.

My older brother Jerry appeared angry for many years as well. His channeling of anger was mostly toward our parents and family as a whole. Jerry could not stand Dad for the most part, and would engage in heated arguments more often than not. I really can't remember participating in a family gathering where the two of them got along that well. Jerry was a perfectionist and completely set in his ways, rarely giving in or admitting any error on his part for most issues related to the family or otherwise. I believe this was his way of channeling anger in a less than constructive way directed at his family, but he was never violent. In my opinion, his was a need to vent at every opportunity to attempt at making long standing points about resolving past issues and getting some respect as the elder sibling and leader. I don't believe any of us, including our parents, had enough patience to allow him the latitude for venting effectively. Instead we retreated and distanced ourselves from him as the years went by. Jerry seems to be calmer these days following his decision to separate and become estranged from most family members, especially parents.

Mother seemed to become angrier with age. She didn't get along with anybody, including friends or family very well. She would strike with her wrath consistently to build herself up and to put down others. Divide and conquer seemed to be the strategy. Pit one against the other was her way for many years. Talking incessantly with little or no listening skills was apparent most of the time. She would easily shut down if challenged and become extremely angry and defensive.

My brother Dan demonstrated anger for many years. Danny was always the tough guy who was going to kick everybody's ass to solve problems. In fact, he almost got himself killed when his son, Branden, got in a fight while they were driving home some years back. Branden got out of the car to pick a fight with another driver, so my brother got out of the car to throw his weight around and both of them ended up in the hospital with stab wounds. Danny seemed to calm down after this incident, but to this day he has a tough guy attitude, even at age 64. I don't think he could fight his way out of a paper bag now, but you would think he is ready to participate in a gang fight any moment. My brother Danny loves a good fight to this day. He had his share of fighting during teenage years and it seemed to be the way he expressed his anger at that time.

My younger brother Scott and sister, Laura, also have experiences that support using anger as a destructive response. They were also subjected to inter-generational transfer of PTSD symptoms due to the prolonged exposure to toxic family living. Both have had their emotional challenges over the years, including alcohol and drug abuse and self destructive behaviors. All siblings appear to have had severe emotional issues for most of their lives, either due to the toxic family culture or other environmental issues. There is no one in our family that we could say experienced typical or normal behavior. This is a very sad statement of fact to share, but still true. All of us seem to have survived in our own ways and have lived relatively productive and successful lives, even with all of the baggage born through being raised in a highly toxic family culture. But since my residence as a writer is Depoe Bay, Oregon, I'm reminded of the famous movie, starring Jack Nicholson, "One Flew over the Cuckoo's Nest" was filmed here locally many years ago. You do the math!

Controlled use of Alcohol as a Medication

This would suggest that alcohol is a good thing for a person with PTSD symptoms. Not so, the only difference I can see is that those of us who have used alcohol to numb the pain did it more or less in a controlled way, i.e., "5 o'clock somewhere." But my experience with alcohol was far from positive, especially after hours.

Thanks to my loving wife, Judy, my drinking days ended almost 11 years ago and it saved my marriage. I was a "5:00 p.m. somewhere drunk." My drinking hours lasted between 5pm-8pm every day of my adult life until age 55. During that time I was taking pain medications due to a diagnosis of severe debilitating osteoarthritis. I could barely walk and was planning to replace my right knee joint along with surgery on my left foot to fuse bones and to fix a collapsed arch. I was also looking at replacing my right shoulder joint as well. This was a painful time both emotionally and physically. The condition basically ended my career in the IT business and made me disabled to the extent that I could no longer keep up with any kind of extensive travel or walking that was mandatory in a highly competitive and demanding outside sales and marketing role. I was advised to stop drinking primarily due to taking these medications. But since it was a well established lifestyle that I looked forward to each day, it was almost impossible to stop drinking. I thought, like all drunks who think they can control it, that it was okay. Besides it helped me forget about facing some tough emotional issues at the time.

I became a different person while drinking alcohol and taking medications at the same time. My emotional disposition exploded and could not be controlled. I became angry most of the time and there were many dinner time outbursts at my wife and daughter. I have to admit that drinking started to become a tougher issue to deal with anyway as the aging process took hold. My doctor advised me that there is a window of opportunity for drinkers like me. "Stop by the time you are 55 or quitting becomes exponentially more difficult and is often a death sentence for men or women in their early to mid 60's." Then shortly after that the big smack on the head came just in time.

One evening at dinner I experienced a complete over the top outburst of anger at Judy and daughter, Sarah. I exploded with hate and total disregard and disrespect for my family. I was so mad, and drunk, flight was the only answer. I left home and drove away for about two hours, then came home. Judy would not let me back in the house. She finally agreed to come out and talk to me on the swinging bench on our porch.

We had been living in the beautiful Icicle Valley near Leavenworth, Washington, for over 10 years. We made a decision in 1990 to relocate to a smaller town in the mountains and build our dream log home. I had huge success at Nortel Networks during my career, so we had a "war chest" to get a new start. Judy wanted to pursue her early childhood teaching career.

We wanted a new life in a small town to raise Sarah who was 3 years old when we moved from Atlanta, Georgia, to Leavenworth, Washington. It was a beautiful thing, and my family was the best thing that ever happened to me. Judy made a huge difference in my life. I felt unconditional love for the first time in my life. I began to feel what it was like to actually love someone and experience intimacy the way one sort of dreams about. Judy and Sarah helped me to become a grounded person and showed me how to build a loving family and meaningful life in paradise. We were not aware at the time that there was something else going on with me that did not surface until recently when doing the research on this book. The PTSD symptoms were exacerbated dramatically with alcohol and medications at the same time. I was about ready to throw all this out the window when the light came on.

When Judy looked me in the eyes and said that she would leave me if I didn't stop drinking, I was shocked. From that point 11 years ago forward and to this day, our 27th anniversary, April 21, 2011, alcohol has not been part of my life. There was no way I would give up the best thing that ever happened to me in my life. And the days ahead got better and better. The medications worked to help me with pain and were also beneficial to me with my PTSD symptoms. Severe arthritis has a side benefit for me since this condition often causes depression and anxiety; my medications include the right prescriptions for both pain and anxiety. I kept my promise to Judy and to Sarah not to drink anymore. They both have supported me 100% and helped me through the early part of the transition. But basically, I just quit and with the help of therapy, I fortunately did not have to deal with some of the addiction problems that alcoholics must address. I was lucky. I do think unconditional love has been a strong enough motivation to give me that extra strength to recover and to stay strong.

I've known most of my life about the damaging effects of alcohol. I've seen it in other people, including my father and other family members. Alcohol is a depressant and causes a person to fly off the handle and become angry more easily. I was already angry due to PTSD symptoms and didn't really need help from alcohol. Being angry is mostly something in my past these days. I rarely feel angry anymore. I am still intense about my work and focus on passionate beliefs, but angry no more. What a gift! From my experience, living with anger is the worst horror one can have in life. Reconciliation and forgiveness as a matter of human behavior or religious beliefs does bring peace of mind. My life is peaceful these days. Each day has its challenges, but it is so much easier to manage my life without anger and fear. I wake up each morning with the gift of unconditional love and go to bed at night with the same feelings. I look forward to each day with my loving soul mate, Judy, and the opportunities to spend with friends and family, and in giving back to the community.

Alcohol appeared to exacerbate my Dad's angry outbursts and behavior as well. My brother Jerry recalls Dad as being relatively calm when he first came home from the war. He drank, of course, and partied, but seemed okay for the most part. But as time passed, Dad started drinking more and staying out late at the CPO club. He was given shore duty for awhile and was running the brig at the Oak Knoll Naval Hospital near San Francisco right after the end of WWII. Tension started after Mother became pregnant with me in the fall of 1945. He would frequently come home late and launch into an angry outburst at Mother and slap Jerry around. He liked to hit kids on the head for some reason. According to Jerry, Dad acted like another child competing for attention with Mother. He was basically jealous of his son who he never bonded with since he was gone so long in the war.

My brother Jerry tells the story of my Dad coming home late from the CPO club one night when we later lived in Navy housing in San Diego, California. Dad was assigned to train boots at the Naval Training Center during that period. Dan and I were ages 1 & 2 respectively at the time and were in bed sleeping. Mother was so mad at Dad that she literally "beat the shit out of him" when he started acting out. She pulled him up the stairs, according to Jerry, continuing her rage and beating on him relentlessly. Finally, she put him in bed and settled down. Jerry said he felt kind of good about this event, but my view is that it is highly damaging for a young boy to witness this kind of violence, which probably had a lingering emotional effect on him during his life. In the book, ***Ghosts from the Nursery***, research shows that when small children and babies observe violence it has a direct and negative effect on brain development. Unborn children can actually acquire certain symptoms connected with PTSD that start to show up later, possibly not serious, but the symptoms can appear.

Research suggests that certain men coming home from the war had a difficult time adjusting to social life and normal family interactions. Dad never hit Mother, but did seem to take his anger out on us kids, starting with Jerry. It was over the top in terms of exceeding what could be categorized as a normal type spanking. When Dad was drunk, he would hit

Jerry and slap him around pretty hard, and that caused Mother to defend her son. This made Dad worse and he felt rejected and misplaced after being out to sea fighting for over two years. According to the medical research approximately 10% of veterans returning from the war at that time, especially those that experienced battle or had been diagnosed with "battle fatigue", did not adjust well and eventually demonstrated angry and bad behavior toward family members, including using alcohol in excess. Jerry always said that Dad acted much better without excessive use of alcohol, but was still defensive and on the edge most of the time. Jerry became withdrawn and fearful of Dad after awhile and there was never any real bonding between the two.

It's easy to say now that if only some of the medications for anxiety would have been available things might have been easier to manage with Dad at the time. The medications would have helped Mother as well. But what we had at the time was alcohol, easily available providing short term relief, but disastrous long term effects with excessive daily use. This was clearly true in my experience with alcohol. Once I stopped drinking it was easier, but I was taking various anxiety and anti-depressant medications to help me. Dad did not have this sort of treatment at the time and would never admit the need to meet with a psychiatrist. He was too proud, and the least path of resistance was alcohol.

Emotional Numbing- the "Hurt Locker"

As my story unfolds and discovery leads the way to a better understanding of my own behavior over the years, I am now saddened to learn how much others were hurt along the way. In my condition, many friends and family members, and the closest ones, fell victim to my outward inability to cope or to control my behaviors. Effectively, I hurt people, friends and family from the past, including former wives and my dear children. I didn't hurt them physically, but certainly emotional abuse was in the mix. I was "numb" to the effects and consequences of my actions toward others. I was unable to control my behavior to the extent that mitigating my actions was even possible. I'm not alone in failed marriages in the world, but I could have managed these situations far better than I did to lessen the already inherent emotional stress of breaking up families. I basically took "flight" leaving carnage in my path. I would not or could not take the time, or had the patience, nor the compassion to engage in these life changing events in a responsible way.

I may have been "numb" on the surface, but I'm now able to attribute the "perpetual anxiety" referred to earlier as my mind and body rejecting these hurtful behaviors. I'm still seeking and hoping for forgiveness, but do have realistic expectations. I can't change the past but my life today is all about giving to others and making amends. My goal is to leave this world at peace, as much peace as anyone who has hurt many others can achieve through the reconciliation process. The ability to go back and find all the wrongs, understand them and my own actions and reasons behind them, gives me the strength to make a difference in the lives of others, starting with my own family and close friends, including giving back through community service. I have lots to give back and refuse to sit around feeling sorry for myself and not sharing my blessings of talents, gifts, and skills to help others achieve their life goals, especially our kids who need mentoring , love, and support the most.

Memory Loss is Troubling

My brothers and sister would often tell more over the years that my memory appeared to be absent of many childhood and teenage year's events as compared to them. Writing this book and doing research on both the implications of PTSD on my behaviors in life as they are connected to a toxic family environment has been revealing. There are both clinical and empirical data showing that my experience as a victim of prolonged abuse as a child and stress related incidents well into my teenage years as a young adult has had a dramatic effect on my memory.

Probably the most troubling memory issue is a 6-8 month period during my time in the US Navy at age 18-19, which is discussed earlier in this story. This event connected with falling in love with Sheryl in Hawaii, leading to a marriage commitment and becoming a "runaway groom" the night before the wedding, is a foggy period of memory at best. My conclusion now is this particular experience was so traumatic for me that my mind blocked it out for the most part as my life came back together. I know now, according to my sister Laura's recollection that Dad succeeded in beating me down to a point where I must have believed that this marriage was not the right thing to do. But the cowardly act of not confronting the situation directly with Sheryl and her family myself apparently made me feel extremely guilty and remorseful to the extent that I suffered a complete emotional breakdown, leading to my early honorable discharge from the Navy.

There are many situations as a child, including recently being reminded while visiting the Grand Canyon in the summer of 2011. I called my brother Danny and started telling him, "it was sure good to see the Grand Canyon again in my later years since as a child traveling west from Minnesota; my memory was not very good at all." My brother quickly jumped on me to say that we never did get to the Grand Canyon, so this was actually my first visit! He went on explain the entire episode in detail. I had absolutely no recollection of these details as my brother recalled them to me. The part I should have remembered to be sure was how Danny covered up the car door window that broke apart because he slammed the door so hard. Since the windows were rolled down due to the heat anyway, Dan got away with abusing our new vehicle, a 1957 Chevy. Danny knew that Dad would have beaten him up in his customary way as brutal as it could be. The broken window was discovered when we arrived in Los Angeles, and Dad fixed it believing the heat on the trip had something to do with the glass breaking.

The clinical research shows that stress caused by abuse or combat or a terrible accident where others are killed, can cause partial or complete memory loss and is clearly a symptom of PTSD.

"Studies in animals showing glucocorticoid-mediated hippocampal toxicity and memory dysfunction with stress raised the question: Does early stress, such as childhood abuse, result in similar deficits in human subjects? With this in mind, we used neuropsychological testing to measure declarative memory function in PTSD. We selected measures that were validated in studies of patients with epilepsy to be specific probes of hippocampal function. These neuropsychological measures (including delayed paragraph recall and word list learning) were correlated with a loss of neurons in the hippocampus in patients who underwent surgical resection of the hippocampus for the treatment of epilepsy.[20] We initially found verbal declarative memory deficits using similar measures in Vietnam combat veterans with PTSD.[21]"

I am beginning to patch together my memory, but it is extremely difficult, requiring the assistance of my family and potentially clinical experts who specialize in amnesia. I continue to be conflicted on how healthy it is to dig up the past this way, but I'm encouraged by experts in the field that it is the right thing to do. I do feel some sense of relief as the pain of some of the events come back to me, but thinking about any of this is scary, especially the risk of remembering something really terrible that may have happened during my early childhood years.

Can polio affect early child brain development?

As a follow up note to memory loss implications, it should not be a minor detail that I contracted polio at two years of age. The Polio virus along with other viral infections can affect the nervous system according to research data and cause certain mental disorders and developmental delays in children. I have been motivated over the years to understand how the polio virus may have made me more susceptible to the effects of stress on brain chemistry. The trauma connected with child abuse clearly causes extreme stress on a child's brain chemistry according to early childhood research. With polio in the mix while growing up in a toxic home, my brain may have been more sensitive to the stress than my siblings. Another significant factor is the current research connected with Post Polio Syndrome (PPS). Some symptoms of polio appear to surface years after a person recovers from the initial effects of the polio virus. All of us have experienced the symptoms of PTSD, but my experience has been far more evident than with my brothers and sister. Virtually all of the symptoms of PTSD have surfaced in more serious ways in my case and are discussed in this story. Now in my mid 60's with many valuable life experiences, I have the ability to make adjustments and manage my PTSD symptoms more effectively, including taking certain medications to help with chronic anxiety.

References:

http://scholar.google.com/scholar?q=impact+of+polio+on+early+child+brain+development&hl=en&as_sdt=0&as_vis=1&oi=scholart

http://www.ncf-net.org/conference/firstwold.htm

http://en.wikipedia.org/wiki/Poliomyelitis

Looking to be "born again" with big life changes

A new beginning in Leavenworth, Washington was to be a blessing.

I've always had this feeling that my life would be cut short somehow along the way, and had a sense of urgency to move fast and make it big news. Cutting my career short and moving to the beautiful mountains surrounding Leavenworth, Washington in 1990, was a monster move! During the late 80s my career with Nortel Networks in the information technology industry was at an unbelievable high point. I really didn't deserve all this success. I was born and raised in a "second class" home for starters. Why did I deserve to become a vice president of sales of a Fortune 500 company making well into a six figure income, living in a 5000 square foot home near the Atlanta Golf and Country Club in Duluth, Georgia? Well, I worked my ass off and pushed people around and out of the way to succeed. I finally graduated from college with a BA in Management from St. Mary's College in Moraga, Ca. I was married to Judy, a beautiful blue eyed, petite, sexy, athletic and adventurous lady who loved to take a calculated risk with me. I was fortunate to have another chance at being a father with the adoption of our little girl, Sarah, who changed our lives completely. I was on the fast track and had to somehow get the hell out and take advantage of our dream to build a log home and live in the mountains before life ended. This was the kind of sense of urgency and PTSD symptom that moved me for many years, until starting life over and learning how to slow down in a small town tucked away in the beautiful Icicle Valley about two miles from town. And life begins again with a surreal feeling of being someplace very special to share with my family, including our loving dog Sadie. Sadie, a yellow Labrador retriever, was tired of airplanes and relocating from one place to another. She would come to love the wide open spaces of Icicle Valley, especially playing in the snow with Sarah and swimming in the Icicle River.

It was a big challenge getting our log home built from a distance. We picked a log home contractor from Oregon, who turned out to be a crook. It was the first time I experienced neighbors and friends coming together to help each other in a small town. Other contractors in the Leavenworth area came to our rescue and became close friends as we settled in our new home during the coldest winter ever with subzero temperatures and tons of snow. This wonderful place in the mountains close to a popular little Bavarian community was like being close to God. The air was so fresh and clean, giving me a feeling of freedom and living life on my own terms. I was done with all the politics of being a corporate executive, endlessly on the road trying to make my numbers. Beating people up trying to make it happen gets to you after awhile. I didn't like being referred to as "the biggest asshole in the company who makes shit happen." It was time to move on with a war chest that made it much easier to start a new life.

Judy's dream of living in a log home in the mountains came true as well. Sarah and our dog Sadie loved it too.

The reader can easily see that my life living with PTSD is full of "sense of urgency" bold and risky moves and decisions. I now know why, but it does not cause me to wish returning and changing past events since certain decisions have made me who I am and there are good lessons learned in the mix. One aspect that is truly important in all of this is having a spouse and life partner like my loving wife, Judy. Judy is the kind of partner and soul mate who loves romance and adventure. She is sort of conservative, but wants to live her dreams just like me. She has, however, given me a check and balance component that keeps me from falling off a cliff in the process of being "reborn" more often than most folks. I can remember the early days of our dating skiing in the Cascades. Judy was a great downhill skier, and I was clearly intermediate or less. She pushed me to ski better and go for the double black diamond challenge that scared me away in the past. Judy would jump off a snow ledge on top and ski down like a bandit and stand there waiting for me to come down, waving her hands and blowing kisses in the wind. I went for it big time. I wasn't about to be left stranded on top of the mountain at Crystal near Tacoma, and let this pretty thing get away from me. So I jumped off and went for it, but not without many falls and hurt muscles for a long time. Once getting down to Judy I was rewarded with a big hug and long delicious kiss. What better motivation can you give a young guy who is completely and insanely in love with this wonderful and beautiful woman, Judy Lee Young? Still deeply in love, I feel very lucky to this day almost 30 years later, to have Judy as my lifetime soul mate.

At the very least I thought my career path had ended with Nortel Networks, and hanging out in the mountains in early retirement was my next move. Not so; head hunters started calling me right away. Six months after moving to Leavenworth and getting settled in our new life, I found myself interviewing with the CEO of Applied Voice Technology (AVT) in Kirkland, Washington. He was recruiting a new sales vice president to come in and help build a distribution channel strategy for the company. This was the last thing on my mind a few weeks earlier when the call came in, and suddenly excitement won me over.

A few weeks later, I accepted an offer to join AVT as their new vice president, distribution sales, following more interviews with other executives in the company and a board member. I had to do it! My career was in my blood after over 35 years, so my rationalization was that returning to the fast paced technology business was part of my retirement transition. But something happened just before starting my new job that gave me a signal that did not keep me from going back to work. I suffered a grand mal seizure at home the Thursday before starting my new job the following week. I almost bit off my tongue during this first time episode, but was able to recover enough to start work anyway. After all the testing and starting on a seizure control medication, my doctor told me that major life changes in a short period of time may have been the cause since the MRI did not show anything troubling in my brain region nor did the blood tests show anything out of normal ranges. I could have been dehydrated since it was hot during that time and we were still working on completing our home. I am convinced to this day that my excessive use of alcohol at the time caused this event as a result of being dehydrated. But who knows, and it certainly didn't keep me from jumping into the snake pit again, getting back to endless travel, making the numbers, and being an asshole again.

The big surprise returning to work was reporting to the vice president of marketing who did not like me. I believe the CEO wanted to break me in and used his marketing VP as my coach for awhile as my feet got wet in the new job. This was a bad decision from the start. The two of us didn't get along at all. Consequently, six months later after putting up with lots of old crap left behind at Nortel Networks and missing my family deeply, I resigned from AVT and returned to a more peaceful life in the mountains. I even rented an apartment in Kirkland to be closer to the job during the week and would go home on the weekends. It was not a mistake to take this position because it helped me realize that my family and a different future were far more important than being a high flying executive in the information technology business.

The AVT experience would not be the end of my career. I was able to find consulting work from time to time for a number of years, eventually returning to Nortel Networks in 1999 and working from my home in Leavenworth for a couple of years before retiring completely as a result of a company reorganization. I then returned to consulting work for a couple of years until mobility issues forced me into retirement. Severe osteoarthritis took its toll on my joints, requiring bone fusion surgeries and joint replacements to keep me on my feet. Although there are no regrets, my body was abused with a high level athletic life style and bad genes. I would not change all the fun over the years of surfing, skiing, hiking, running, and playing sports during most of my adult life. I was very good at falling off ladders and buildings as well. It became clear to me that taking care of my body and pursuing less risky physical activities had to become a much higher priority while progressing through the 50's age bracket.

The most interesting part of our experience in Leavenworth was getting into the retail business. Judy and I purchased Northwest Gourmet in 1993. I was already doing consulting work and getting involved in the community at the time, so buying or starting a business was viewed as an opportunity to put our stake in the ground in a small community. We turned Northwest Gourmet into a popular retail specialty food and coffee house. Espresso was really starting to kick in at the time and we only had one or two other coffee shops in town.

Becoming a Leavenworth business owner gave me an introduction to politics and a chance to get involved in a non-profit, Leavenworth's famous "Art in the Park." Although owning a small business is a huge challenge and community service was highly rewarding, we struggled with the business after the first year following the big fires of 1994. Leavenworth, as a resort destination town, was closed down for several weeks and business essentially died and never came back the same. While in Lake Tahoe with Sarah visiting my brother Danny, I watched in horror as the mountains all around our home burned. Judy called me and asked me to come home because everyone was being evacuated. Our home was relatively safe since we lived in the middle of Icicle Valley and far enough away from the high density tree lines.

We barely broke even with Northwest Gourmet until selling in 1996 to a local coffee roaster who needed retail space. This was clearly one of those "bold" decisions to be "reborn" that certainly provided us with a character building experience and a moderate income for a few years. Judy was well on her way with her re-energized early childhood teaching career so we did make ends meet and were able to get out of this business without sustaining a big loss. Both Judy and Sarah helped me with the business along the way. It was hard work but rewarding most of the time. I felt bad at times since Judy was working her day job and then helped me on weekends. Holidays and festivals were big business for Leavenworth. I'll never forget our first Christmas Tree Lighting Festival in 1993 when we sold almost 500 lattes in one day! I became a barista with the best of them in the espresso business at that time. It was fun having a reputation for making the best coffee in town.

No doubt on top of my list of highly interesting professional and personal experiences was working for a family owned printing technology business. SBI for short, as we later included in the company name, was located out in the Chumstick Valley about 8 miles from town. I came to know this highly energetic entrepreneur family from my experience in Village Art in the Park. The matriarch of the family, Nadine, was on the board and also CEO of SBI. After I returned from my Applied Voice Technology stint, Nadine asked me to come in and help her company find their way in the context of business and strategic planning. I knew nothing about the printing business, but soon learned and as a bonus, discovered a whole new loving friendship with a wonderful dysfunctional, creative, and eccentric family with Moritz as the head master of this clan, so he thought. Nadine was really the most stable of them all and clearly running the business, and a blessing it was too. The adult children, Jim and Mary, needed to learn how to take over the company as well, so this became a more subtle part of my new assignment. SBI did not have a succession plan, and needed one badly. Jim and Mary worked in the business since they were very young. Both were highly educated and clearly had leadership qualities, especially Mary, who later became CEO when her mother Nadine sadly passed away. This was a highly emotional and transitional time for the family. Moriitz was a genius and challenging to work with at times, but was a wonderful and highly sensitive person to know.

My career work was definitely consistent with all the experience and skills needed to help SBI, and my own dysfunctional life living with PTSD turned out to be an advantage working with this unique entrepreneurial family. It was very difficult for the family to communicate with others, including each other, which resulted in a huge challenge of attracting talented professionals to work with them on a consistent basis. This was a job that fit nicely into my profile and leadership qualities, including significant experience working with creative and often times emotionally driven people with lots of hang ups. There was no lack of intellectual capital in this family, however. They just needed some business disciplines to move SBI to a higher level of success. SBI's Moritz invented the egg carton printer many years ago and had a corner on the market, but competition was beginning to appear in the market, especially overseas. The business was steady and had moderate growth for all these years until competition begin to show its strength, especially in the spare parts space. It was a fun and rewarding, but often frustrating experience working with the family, but will always be a most memorable period in my working life. Friendship with the SBI family was the most rewarding outcome. It was very sad when Nadine passed away from cancer around 2000 shortly after my Dad died. This is when the succession plan started to pay off and Mary and Jim finally took over the business and clearly preserved the family legacy to this day. Moritz eventually retired but maintained an as needed role in the company. The SBI family business experience is an excellent example of how critical it is for a small business to have a succession plan.

How does any of this relate to PTSD symptoms? Most of it does since it might be hard to find anyone normal who has had this sort of crazy experience leaving a high paying career in the IT industry, moving to the mountains, becoming a retail business owner in a small town, and leading a non-profit organization. A logical and educated person would not normally take all this on unless there was a sense of urgency about life ending at any moment and the need to experience everything life has to offer right now and without hesitation. Do I believe all of this makes sense? Not at all, but the adventure and romance from a subjective standpoint makes all the sense in the world. Ask Judy and Sarah… My reading audience may draw their own conclusions as well.

Mother & Dad in 1989 with a cougar

Mom & Dad happy times during the mid to late 1980s

**Dad circa 1964 receiving Officer of the Year award during his
career with the Federal Correctional Institution**

PART III

LESSONS LEARNED

What did we learn from this amazing journey?

My initial decision to write this story was based on communicating more effectively with my family about myself and my experiences. It really got my attention when daughter, Bianca, expressed that she really didn't know me that well nor did her children. Writing has always been a joy, especially as a way to gather information about subject matters and issues that require problem solving and solutions. My entire career, skill sets, and education have taught me how to do a "situation analysis" to capture the essence of matters related to human behavior. I've always been curious about how people behave under various circumstances, and to understand human nature. And in writing this story, these skills came in handy at this point in my life when looking at how we all got here together as a family and as friends. Now is the time to capture what was learned in this research process, and provide ideas and recommendations to help my own family and others as we all attempt to find our way through life. Most importantly, it is an opportunity for me to summarize my own learning experience while writing and researching the subject of intergenerational PTSD. It is a journey to be sure, and an amazing one at that. I believe it is a work in progress providing me a foundation to build on and learn from the rest of my life.

Separating the behavior from the person

My wife and best friend Judy explained the idea of separating the person from the behavior some years ago and has since brought it up from time to time. She was and still is very good at putting behavior in perspective while keeping the person she loves in their original form. I am just beginning to understand how effective and critical it is to do the same with my parents and others in general. It is not easy whatsoever to pull this off, but it becomes easier with practice. The key is to really know the person, and never forget why you loved them initially and still love them today.

I am now able to forgive my parents for their abusive and less than loving behaviors as parents, and at the same time respect them as individuals who lived through some challenging historical times and did not have the education to know and understand the implications of raising children. I am also able to see clearly how a mental health condition can completely change the way a person behaves if treatment is not available or is not pursued. My Dad's personality changed completely from many months of combat duty during his naval career. He was officially diagnosed at the end of WWII with what we now know as a severe case of PTSD. His only treatment was 6 weeks in a mental institution completely isolated from the outside world. God only knows what he went through in terms of the various treatments at the time, including using shock therapy. The medications offered today for anxiety and depression did not exist at that time. The medical professionals released Dad back to duty and believed he would be okay after treating and observing him for 6 weeks. I know Dad's personality, and can easily see how he would be motivated to do everything possible to get back to his Navy life and to be with his family. He was not well when released from treatment at the US Naval Hospital in Oakland, California. His condition was stable but not for long as he got back into normal activities in the Navy as well as family contact. He used alcohol as a medication, which now we know is a depressant and makes symptoms of PTSD far worse, even threatening to family members and others.

Mother, on the other hand, was suffering from severe mental health issues as well, but did not recognize or admit her condition since she was primarily concerned about her husband who returned from war after so many months and years. Mother's goal was to get her husband, Vernon well again so that he could live a productive and happy life following the war. Mother experienced mental health damage and suffered PTSD symptoms from both the depression era and later, the effects of WWII as a spouse, waiting at home for her husband to return, if he returned alive at all. Kids were secondary in my view because parents at that time were constantly distracted by their own personal challenges. Consequently, the symptoms of PTSD would eventually take shape in the behavior of children, unbeknownst to parents or society as a whole at the time.

It took many years for society to change its attitude toward mental health. It was not until the Vietnam War and returning combat veterans who suffered the same symptoms as WWII combat veterans with "battle fatigue," that

Post Traumatic Stress Disorder (PTSD) was discovered as a serious mental health issue related to traumatic experiences, including combat. Post Vietnam era severe trauma became recognized as an invisible wound that appeared first on the battle field and subsequently in the behavior of veterans returning home from combat duty. Severe depression and anxiety began taking its toll until new and better treatments were discovered; especially certain medications that allowed victims to become more stable and therefore begin longer term treatment methodologies.

To this day, however, families have the biggest challenge in living with PTSD since it can be transferred to family members through the abusive behavior of a parent returning from combat duty. The challenge of a spouse and children is to put the abusive behavior in perspective so that the affected parent can make a transition to good mental health without destroying the family unit. Consequently, family members must become educated far in advance of the return of a parent from combat duty. Tough as it is, even with preparation, becoming educated on mental health issues in general provides some relief and hope to families and can strengthen family unity rather than tearing it apart forever. My family is a good example of a completely dysfunctional and less than loving clan that could have done so much better if we had the right kind of treatment and education from the beginning. It is never too late, but trying to bring the family together later in life once we became more knowledgeable and insightful is very difficult if not impossible.

Healing also requires someone inside or outside of the family to intervene by creating an atmosphere of positive communications through talking and/or writing as in this case. For the first time in many years, I am communicating with all my siblings in more positive and constructive ways. Mother, Marcella, at age 93 is even engaged. It is not perfect, and Dad is gone, but we hope finding peace to some extent is now far more realistic than in the past. Writing this story has become a healing process for extended family members as well. Our own spouses and children really didn't understand until recently all the Sparks family dysfunction for so many years. My own children really have not had a chance to get to know me better until now, long after they have been adults, raising their families and going through life experiences themselves. Since writing this story, I have become a much happier person and mostly at peace. This experience has helped me see an even better relationship evolve with my loving wife and children as well. They seem to see me in a different light and hopefully a bigger and better story shines through to them now that they know me better as a person and father. I have developed more patience in my professional work and interactions with close friends and others as well. Living in peace is a wonderful gift, especially as one enters the golden years.

Mitigating self-destructive behavior

This is where we survivors of PTSD have a high risk of crossing the line the most with family members and in professional life. The attitude of "I don't deserve to be happy or successful" is a fallacy. The tendency to punish self grows out of early childhood abuse because children tend to blame themselves when things go wrong at home. Consequently, later in life following a successful experience at work or on the personal level, we can often punish ourselves again and again. We don't seem to have the capacity to forgive ourselves even if intellectually it is clear that whatever happened during early life at home was not your fault.

My brother, Scotty, continues to blame himself for the bad behavior and example of our parents while he was a kid. I believe now he is beginning to learn how to mitigate the feeling that he needs to be punished and will have the opportunity to return to his professional life without the worry of becoming his worst enemy in the middle of a successful endeavor.

The last time I experienced self-destructive behavior was in my early 50's when working as a consultant in Wenatchee, Washington. While participating in an awesome project developing new business strategy for a small IT company, I became extremely angry and walked away because of the perception of being misled and lied to by the principals of the company. I used the platform to release the anger I held mostly for myself for not seeing what was happening with respect to my role following being hired as a new executive in the company. In retrospect, I could have managed this encounter and experience with much more grace and professionalism by negotiating my position in constructive discussions. All I did was return to being an abused child and acted out with an adult tantrum. Sure, the intensity of the business environment and stress could have had something to do with my behavior, but it was not justified. I did a great job punishing myself and exiting the situation. As a result I didn't get the benefit of the follow-on success of executing a well thought out strategic plan for the company while growing into a new executive team member. I was able to "pick up the pieces" again and move on but to this day, I know that my behavior was unacceptable and the outcome could have been highly positive.

Seek help and advice when self-destructive behavior is recognized by your peers or family members. We need to practice recognizing the symptoms of counterproductive behavior, and back off and take a deep breath. Walk away and return the next day with an agenda designed to resolve the conflict in a positive, mature manner.

The biggest lesson learned over the years is that anger is my worst enemy. Anger solves nothing and only escalates unless it is translated into a constructive dialogue where parties feel rewarded with a positive outcome, including specific actions and mutual responsibility.

Unconditional Love

My daughter, Bianca, wrote a letter to her sister, Sarah, on her wedding day a few years ago that really puts the topic in perspective for me.

> *I truly didn't understand unconditional love until I met your mother. We had our difficult times like most families but most importantly, I always knew she loved my sister and me because we were our father's children. Through the difficult times your mother always went above and beyond to encourage, support and help to strengthen our relationship with our father. It meant the world to me and gave me strength and hope knowing that I was not alone anymore. God brought your mother into my father's life not only to bring him back into our lives but also bless us with a sister and bring our family closer than ever before. I couldn't have asked for a more loving and caring wife for my father, stepmother, or grandmother for my children. Your mother was the link that was missing in our father's life and you were a blessing from God that completed our family.* —Bianca Cavello

I was raised in a toxic family culture that didn't know or understand the concept of unconditional love. We grew up without trust in family members or others for that matter. We didn't know love or know how to love. Love had mostly to do with a surface idea that was more physical than spiritual. We were suspect at everything and everybody while growing up and well into our adult lives with some failed marriages and tragic events that go along with the lack of knowing love and trust in others.

I discovered unconditional love with my wife Judy for the first time in my life. What a gift to share with loved ones, especially your spouse. True love will get you through anything, even the most challenging events in life. Having trust in love provides peace and security in life. You know with the feeling of unconditional love that your spouse or other loved ones are always there for each other no matter what gets in the way. You are united as one, sharing in the joy and the sadness that comes during this one-time journey through life. I believe in the end unconditional love allows you to live in peace and rest in peace.

It makes me feel very happy to know that Bianca has unconditional love in her own life and can equally extend her feelings to our family as a whole. I'm hopeful that all my daughters feel unconditional love from not only me but all their loved ones.

Cognitive Response to Severe Trauma

Clinical research and my own experiences, including studying the subject matter in some detail with this story, shows that the human brain must make huge adjustments in wiring to adapt to and mitigate the long term effects of severe trauma. Prolonged exposure to combat in war is a good example and is the basis for this story, and my father, Vernon's experiences in WWII, including surviving the sinking of the USS West Virginia during the Japanese attack on Pearl Harbor on December 7, 1941. At the beginning of this story, I described my Dad's observation of one of his shipmates "falling back to the deck without his head attached" after looking out a porthole when the Japanese started bombing. In further research my findings included the training of men at war to consider themselves as "dead already" to cope with combat stress. The Marines who landed on Iwo Jima knew they had only a 50/50 chance of survival, so they had to rationalize the event in some way to overcome the extreme fear of taking that step on the beach to complete their mission. You just knew it would be either you or your buddy next to you who would not return. Making the experience even worse is to survive and feel guilty and less than deserving as a survivor. Most were able to make it through the war if they survived only to suffer the symptoms of PTSD when returning home to live a normal and healthy life. Which is worse, getting killed in combat or surviving and spending many years or the rest of your life fighting your feelings of guilt and remorse?

Dad didn't do very well with this circumstance for most of his life following the war. He brought his mental health disorder home to family and friends. Medical professionals did not know what to do with these men following brief treatment and release from various recovery treatment hospitals around the country. The good news is that it is estimated that around 10% of combat veterans suffered from symptoms of PTSD, but still this is a large number, especially when you consider the number of veterans during the entirety of WWII. Many who suffered extreme anxiety and depression in battle committed suicide according to the Department of Defense records. If you pile on the implications of inter-generational PTSD among spouses and children, the legacy of WWII and later wars lives on from one generation to the next. I believe the suffering connected to PTSD is so severe and debilitating that it can be worse than death and definitely compares to the suffering that occurs from a severe physical wound. Although a physical wound can be healed, the victim can still suffer from the symptoms of PTSD for many years if not a life-time.

I know from my own experience as a survivor of inter-generational PTSD that the pain at times is overwhelming and highly challenging to treat and mitigate. In my case, life has felt like a race to get somewhere fast, but never fast enough. If I slowed down for just a moment, the knot in my gut would return bringing on anxiety and the drive to get back into the race to nowhere. I did not know how to relax and be at peace until later in my life. It was not until I could spend most of my time in retirement thinking about others and helping others that the anxiety started to subside. Admittedly, medications to relieve anxiety and depression, if used correctly, have been a huge help to me over the years. I can well understand how brain chemistry can be adjusted to bring relief to symptoms. Having an exercise regimen all my adult life has been a natural medication for relieving symptoms of anxiety and depression as well. The one bad medication to stay away from is alcohol, period.

You can be lost in this world without a good education!

All too often we talk about education in terms of improving a person's intellectual capacity to gain a better competitive position in the work force, whether it is a vocational or academic pursuit. I believe education goes much further than this, and allows a person to achieve a better understanding of human behavior dynamics and the world around us. My enlightenment and discovery of unconditional love did not come until my brain started connecting to deep empathy toward the feelings of loved ones and others around me. I learned about empathy earlier on in the context of my professional life as it relates to putting yourself in the "customer's shoes." But this kind of empathy is about making the sale and professional success. What about empathy on a more personal level with the people you love and close friends? Understanding empathy in a much deeper way didn't come until later in my life, once all the mistakes piled on, including getting past not being reared in a culture of love at home.

Feeling insecure most of the time does not help a person empathize very well. Understanding the customer's needs and applications that add value to a company's bottom line is shallow, but is often referred to as the word "empathy." This type of empathy goes an inch deep at best, and allows a person to maximize the chances of succeeding in the business world, but falls far short in personal life. A good example of shallow empathy in personal life is the way to see your spouse or significant other. If making your wife happy has to do with your physical relationship for the most part, the relationship is headed in the wrong direction. I know this sounds terrible, but this is exactly what happens when a kid does not grow up in a loving environment at home. I had no intellectual or emotional concept of love or empathy in my personal life until knowing my wife, Judy. Our relationship changed everything!

I am proud of my academic and professional achievements, but much happier with achieving profound feelings of empathy toward others at this point in my life. This kind of empathy is a gift from God. It takes years to develop and should start very early in life. Playing catch-up during adult years can have disastrous consequences. I am sometimes in shock to think about how a person even survives for long without a profound sense of empathy. I can only assume that loved ones and close friends had significant emotional empathy toward others, including me. Certainly, Judy is a good example. Otherwise, my life would not have proceeded to a relatively successful point at this later stage. Thank God for all the wonderful and loving people in my life, including my own family, especially Judy and others close to me.

I do not underestimate the importance of education in the context of a person's professional or vocational life, making a decent living, and becoming a self sustaining and productive person in society. To become a well rounded person with the emotional capacity to empathize and love others, however, requires a much higher level of education and exposure to the dynamics of human behavior.

How well do you know your parents?

I do not hold too many positive memories of my childhood. The staging for detachment from mother and father came very early as a child. It was fear that moved me away from both of them. Kids are resilient and continue toward having loving relationships with their parents, however. Siblings take on a similar behavior of distrust and detachment as well. As a result, we see the family running away from each other and avoiding contact as much as possible. A defensive posture of interaction emerges in a toxic culture. If there is no leadership from parents to reverse this trend, it takes on a life of its own. Consequently, kids do not get a chance to know their parents very well at all.

It is difficult, if not impossible, to break the pattern in a toxic culture; and if it does not happen with some kind of well received intervention, we eventually escape from home and move on with our own lives without knowing our parents. It was only recently that I really decided to take the time to find my parents and siblings again and know them better. Knowing mother and dad as real people has been an enlightening experience. Writing this story forced me to look at everything and gather information in the same way that I would do research on any project that motivated me to learn more. Once doing this kind of homework, my whole perspective changed. I started to know my parents better and began understanding where they came from, all the challenges they faced in life, and how they were able or not able to cope with the stresses of life. As this story unfolds, I learned my parents lived a life of extreme stress and pain.

My parents grew up too fast and really didn't have the right foundation for unconditional love in the first place. Nor did they receive the right kind of mentoring and education to gain a broader picture of human behavior and the meaning of empathy, and most importantly, unconditional love. Kids never know what love means unless parents show them early. Not only do parents need to show their children love directly by bonding with them, including lots of appropriate hugging and kissing. Kids need lots of hugging, love and reinforcement to develop their minds and bodies in a healthy way. I used to believe that expressing emotions made me look weak. I had to be tough to survive this toxic environment. Dad was tough and mean, so this is the kind of model many kids can grow up with. In my Dad's case the rigors of military "boot camp" training is not appropriate for a 5 year old child. Common sense suggests that demonstrating leadership as a parent and expressing love toward your children is the right way to parent. Act like a jerk as a parent, and you raise jerks for kids. Modeling appropriate behavior and setting an example by mentoring and doing the right things with children, including lots of encouragement and reinforcement is cool and will go a long way to create a loving family culture and minimize the baggage kids carry with them when leaving home to become a responsible adult.

I'm not sure it would have been possible until now to get to know my parents better. This may be the reality for many children since we are not mature enough as kids to figure out all this fancy strategy and learn about human behavior to connect the dots effectively. I now know my parents far better. The benefits at this late stage are huge. I can now separate the behavior from the person as discussed in this book earlier. Peace is my goal in life at this stage, and it feels good finally to know Mom and Dad much better even though it has taken so long and most of my life to get here. I strongly believe in the statement, "it's never too late." My own experiences suggest strongly and painfully that second chances and even third chances are possible to achieve a better quality of life at an emotional level. The best example of regretting not knowing my Dad as a person was my decision not to attend his memorial service when he passed away in 1998. Writing this book and telling his story is helping me heal from not getting closure earlier in life, especially at the time Dad passed away.

I do feel closer to my parents now, but do not condone their abusive behavior for so many years. As a family we can't go back and change anything, but we can look forward to doing a much better job as parents ourselves by learning from all the mistakes or missteps that happened for many reasons and circumstances that could not be controlled.

Picking up the pieces and moving on

"Failure is not an option." A very close friend, Jack, made this statement sometime ago as it related to our work with Neighbors for Kids, www. neighborsforkids.org. When it gets right down to it, there are things in life that we cannot accept defeat or failure. These are the values we hold dearly, including our emotional and mental health. All of us have a responsibility and duty to do our part to make our world better. But we can't do a very good job helping others if we can't fix ourselves and stay healthy.

Fixing ourselves and staying in good health is not easy and is definitely a work in progress all of our lives. It is shocking to me to discover how being in denial can be a huge challenge in moving forward in constructive ways. I spent lots of time in one to one talks with professionals, learning in college, gaining experience at work, and getting the benefits of a loving relationship at home. It wasn't until my "big secret" was revealed to myself and others that healing really started to take shape. My secret, as described earlier in the story, was the shame and guilt felt by backing off on the "wedding that didn't happen" using my father as the go between, including putting together a story about my crazy emotional condition and breakdown at the time. I'm still struggling to forgive myself, but getting closer. It was especially disconcerting to experience a self-fulfilling prophecy of actually being diagnosed by Navy medical professionals as being "emotionally unstable," later coined Post Traumatic Stress Disorder (PTSD). This diagnosis, leading to an early honorable separation from the Navy, was a tragic event in my life. The experience was completely against my own personal values and character. Memory loss became part of the coping mechanism as well. I am still trying to put the puzzle back together from my 30 day training cruise on the USS Coucal. I might have to wait for writing my next book or use my Blog, www.livingwithptsd-sparkles.blogspot.com to share this mystery with my readers when memory serves. I'm also convinced that trying to contact my ex-fiancé, Sheryl, to apologize is not a good idea. I do not want to risk bringing this hurtful experience back into her life at this stage. This is my problem to resolve not hers. I only wish that Sheryl, a very beautiful and loving person in my past, ended up with all the best in life, including a loving husband and family.

The other tragic event in my life was to leave my children at ages 3 & 5 to move on to a not so healthy relationship with another woman. I do not know if my ex-wife has forgiven me, but I have apologized more than once to my daughters, Deanna and Bianca, and to Lillian as well. I've tried to be a good father over the years and make amends. My wife Judy has helped me tremendously, making our extended family a loving and caring culture. Learning and believing in unconditional love has made family relationships much better. Having grandkids in my life has been the best. Knowing that Judy loves my daughters and grandkids as her own is a gift. Judy has made a world of difference in creating a highly positive relationship with my adult children and grandkids. Our adopted daughter

Sarah is also a blessing in my life and represents a second chance for me to become a better father.

I've had to pick up the pieces and move on, so to speak, in my professional life, but as discussed earlier in this story, it is the values we hold dearly that become most important in life. The career part ends up being a shallow experience without strong personal values and unconditional love and empathy toward others.

Now, later in life, reaching out more with loved ones and friends has become the most effective way to heal emotional wounds of the past. Giving to others, especially through my volunteer work in the community is no doubt, at least for me, a sure bet for maintaining a healthy and happy life. "Picking up the pieces and moving on" is so much easier when reaching out becomes a natural inclination. Although my motivation started with healing old wounds and achieving a healthier and happier life, helping others and serving the community has made my life so much larger than me that there is far less time to become self absorbed. Thinking about others and being highly engaged in the larger community is far more rewarding.

Repairing relationships

It is critical in building stronger relationships or in repairing a troubled relationship, to give or give up something big at the personal level. It is usually something big anyway that one doesn't see right away when relationships go wrong. We usually start compromising with small steps that really only touch the surface of the problem and never really demonstrate a real commitment to change the relationship for the better. In many cases, there is a big trigger event, possibly an accident where someone is hurt, or reaching an emotional crisis that threatens to break up the relationship that really needs the fuel of a personal sacrifice to make a difference. In my case, it was giving up alcohol, which allowed me to become a more compassionate and patient person who spent more quality time listening than being angry and defensive.

In my case, alcohol was the big ticket item on the table with my wife Judy. It was alcohol that prevented me from seeing clearly what was needed to make our marriage much better. I was too defensive and feeling foggy most of the time to really see what was happening. Earlier in this story, I describe the event that allowed me to turn the corner. Judy would leave me if I didn't stop drinking alcohol and taking medications for health issues at the same time. I came to the realization that my marriage was far more important than alcohol and subsequently quit. Life has been better and different in many ways now 11 years after quitting my "5:00 to 8:00 p.m. happy hour" each and every day of the week. Once making the big decision to give up the booze, we were able to move forward. The small steps and promises to be a better partner never worked. I had to give something big, really big, and giving up alcohol was the right move, and it was big.

I also struggled for many years trying to be a good father and build mutually rewarding friendships with my daughters. With my older girls, the damage was huge since I had not been the father at home with them as they grew up. I missed everything in my view, all the good stuff that bonds fathers with daughters. I wasn't there for them when Dad needed to be on hand. My relationship with the youngest daughter, Sarah, was different since we were together as she grew up. But my behavior became intolerable for Sarah as she became a teenager. I didn't set the right example because my anger was out of control; when we clashed it was usually connected with "happy hour."

Sarah came into our life as one of those events that was not a coincidence, causing me to again believe in a higher power. Judy and I wanted to share life with a child and could not make it happen the old fashioned way. Sarah's adoption was a miracle to me. It seemed so natural to have her in our life right from the beginning when we met her 4 hours after she was born. Her birth parents actually picked us out of a portfolio of potential adoptive parents, so it was very special. Sarah showed me how to be a father again and this time it was not confused with my own selfish behaviors and the lack of empathy. I had the time and the desire to be the best Dad in the world. Sarah made me feel special as her Pop and being with her for every little girl event, including her first day of school, was truly a gift to me that will be treasured forever. I felt so lucky to have a second chance at being a father.

I did not do a good job over the years showing unconditional love to all my daughters. They drifted away and my attitude was mostly how it affected me rather than trying to better understand their feelings and needs. Making matters worse with the older girls, they really didn't know me that well, and finally moved on to their own lives when married and starting families.

Since daughter Sarah, the youngest, has been an adult my relationship with her has become very close. I believe the big move on my part was taking alcohol off the table and getting along far better with her mom. She could see directly the changes taking place, and felt more comfortable coming back to the fold, Mom, Dad, and Sarah as a team with unconditional love for each other.

With my older girls, Deanna and Bianca, it continues to be a work in progress, getting better, but slowly with missteps in communications more often than I would prefer. Judy makes a huge difference as their stepmother since my older girls love her dearly. I know they love me, but my efforts to make these relationships better will continue to be a challenge. Leaving them at such an early age and being a distant father has not been the best circumstance to get past. They both feel cheated during their childhood years and no doubt have a hard time considering how their mother was hurt by our divorce. The generational difference between them and younger sister, Sarah, probably causes underlying feelings of envy since Sarah has been part of my life always without any interruptions.

I refuse to fight or argue with them, and consistently take the high road of making every attempt to understand their feelings and listen. I try to show them love and affection as often as possible. I put my ego aside and believe my role is to help and support them in every way possible, but in a responsible way. I remind myself often that parental leadership is what children expect, not sibling-like rivalry or warfare.

Repairing relationships with my brothers and sister, and surviving mother has been much easier since researching and writing this story. Getting them engaged in the process and allowing all of us to learn together by understanding the dynamics and history of our family has improved how we interact in so many ways. Defensive reactions are now breaking down and we listen to each other more. We are learning to separate the difference between the person and behavior, making it easier to see other points of view or look at issues in different ways. We try to focus on our family as a whole working together as a team rather than fighting to hold our respective positions. We are learning to better understand our past experience in a toxic home and to engage in compromise with each other. This is a work in progress to be sure and all of us now seem to be engaged. We do have a ways to go and it will no doubt take the rest of our lives working each day to empathize more with each other.

Although my father has been gone now for over 10 years, I get a sense of closure with him and know that our relationship would be very good now if he were still alive. Having these feelings about Dad has allowed me to heal in a major way. I now know Dad better as a person and as a WWII hero serving his country honorably, which has made a big difference in my attitude. I can talk about my Dad as a person first, then as a parent in a very objective way, especially without anger and resentment and without the whining, complaining and blaming that tends to go with these feelings.

All in all it's a better day, and I feel better about family relationships than at any time in the past.

The spiritual connection

I have never been an extremely religious person, but have always felt a spiritual connection. There have been too many incidents and events that show me that a higher power exists. I have a strong interest in religious studies and keep an open mind about all religions. My conclusion is that most religions are the same and God is much larger than any one religion can represent. Religions represent an opportunity for humans to feel closer to God in a structured and framed way, making it easier to follow and rationalize. I believe this is a good thing for most to find a single religion to hold dearly in their life. For me, my need to understand God goes much further than any religion can offer. I see and feel God in nature and by touching and being close to what is referred to as a "vortex" experience. These are places like the mountains and the ocean or other remote places in the world where life comes together like a symphony and the energy of all this interaction of life feels like God is present.

I also feel God is present at home when the gift of unconditional love is present in my life with my wife Judy each day we are together. I can't see God, but I feel His presence. My relationship with God is a journey through a life of learning and awareness. With each year that goes by, I feel closer to God in a very spiritual and natural way. I have not been able to achieve this sense of spirituality through any religion or in going to church every week. In my view, the subject of God is too big for one specific religion or church to explore in its totality. God is all around us and in everything we see and do. I feel God each day of the week during my own journey in life. I especially feel God and spirituality in the company of my wife, Judy. She is very special to me and gives me hope and guidance each day.

Marriage in itself with unconditional love is clearly a spiritual experience in my view. Life itself is my religious journey and my church too.

The "Me, I" Culture

In a toxic family where PTSD symptoms persist as a result of prolonged abuse and trauma, there is no real family unit. In this environment there is the perception that no one has your back. You are basically alone protecting and defending your turf and position. There is a high level of anxiety and insecurity that grows out of a motivation to survive rather than growing and thriving together as a team with common goals and parental leadership.

I learned something highly important very early in my professional life that was not translated to interactions with family members until many years later. While learning and getting some good coaching in the sales business, the word "I" was considered poison in verbal and written communications. My early career mentors and bosses jumped on me often for using the word "I" as a team member and in working with customers. It was clear from the start that the word "we" carried so much more weight and generated significant positive response once it became a habit to avoid using "I" to reference almost anything. When using "I" it was deliberate and most appropriate at all times. My world changed very quickly in terms of leadership qualities and success in selling once "we" became my favorite word.

In all the years of fighting and arguing with family members and in trying to make my marriage work, including relationships with children, it has been a relatively recent discovery that "we" is most definitely appropriate in building strong relationships at the personal level, especially with family members. It is most noted that when family members focus on themselves in solving problems, nothing constructive ever happens. All my siblings, including parents, and myself have not been team players for most of our lives. I hear the word "I" and "me" far too often, still to this day. It is my sincere opinion that the sooner all of us make the family relationship bigger than ourselves, we will all be on the road to healing and recovery in a more expedient manner. It is so much easier to communicate with people in general when "we" is in context at all times. We are making good progress and in writing this story, it is beginning to become apparent that my brothers and sister think about the value of "we" more now than ever. I definitely dislike hearing the use of "I" most of the time. The reality is that for most things in life it is "we" who develop unconditional love together as a family unit. Unconditional love is not possible in the context of "I."

"The "Me, I, Culture" topic reminds me of the old "locus of control" concept in psychology. Generally speaking, using "I" implies perceiving control as originating with the self. Using "you" turns it away from the self. "I" am in control and powerful, dominating; versus "you" are in control, leaving me helpless. Using "we" dissolves the locus of control illusion by acknowledging the equal and shared responsibility of relationships. "We" encourages dialog and participation so important to healthy relationships." –Byron Lewis

A New Beginning!

Using words like summary for the end of this story seems off the mark. I have a hopeful outlook in writing this book after doing research and connecting the dots. Life can begin again at any stage in life, especially for those of us who are entering the golden years. Writing this story has given me energy, renewed confidence, and a much brighter look into the future. Finding peace of mind has been a huge benefit, but requires continued effort. I believe more now that when one reaches out for answers to big questions and becomes fully engaged in living in a proactive way, we find more peace of mind. My thinking has changed from thoughts of death and dying or old age to planning my next writing project, next adventure, and sharing more romance with Judy. It is never time to sit down and forget about it all. It is extremely healthy for the mind and body to be engaged, to discover, to learn, and to love. Living, learning and loving never ends until the day we actually leave this life for good and go on to the next life, assuming the faith that this is where we are headed.

"Retirement" means transitioning to new beginnings rather than stepping away from all the action. There is really more action in retirement if you are willing to take the leap of faith, and jump in and continue to make a difference in your life and the life of others. The more of my time spent giving to others feels like a gift. Continuing to share my life with soul-mate and wife Judy is comforting and exciting. Finding new friends and building new relationships is invigorating. Getting the most out of participating in the lives of friends and family, including watching my children grow along with the grandkids, is most gratifying. I can say life is as good as it can be as long as my feet stay firmly on the ground. Writing this book clearly represents a new beginning. I am very thankful for having the motivation to tackle this project and the many rewards it has and will produce in the future. I am ready for the next surprise and challenge life has in store for us!

EPILOGUE

Path to Self Discovery – Author's Learning Perspective

In writing this story it became apparent that my own writing style, acquired over the years as a professional, came into play in a most significant way. "Needs Assessment" and "Situation Analysis" has always been a cornerstone of problem solving in terms of leading an organization and in finding solutions to customer needs as well as problem solving. For the purposes of this story and as a useful tool for readers, following is a practical process of self discovery and finding a personal path forward to mitigate mental health challenges and in improving personal or family relationships.

Background

How can you become better prepared for objective and productive consultations with a mental health professional? I have visited with many mental health professionals over the years to little or no avail. Many thousands of dollars and heart ache, including damaged relationships went without solutions because I was either in denial, could not remember, or could not honestly articulate my needs. My discussions and interactions have been about symptoms, not the real problems. We often do this at a professional level, and can more easily find the real problems to solve because of a team environment and focus on quantifiable goals and objectives in the business. You as an individual do not have a team to work with. You are alone trying to figure out complex and subjective issues and pay lots money to seek professional help to find solutions. There are three steps you can take to be better prepared once sitting across from a professional or medical doctor you are just getting to know.

I. Write down your own personal story

Many of the mental health issues start early on in childhood from personal experiences, especially when there is a traumatic event like physical or mental abuse. There could also be a more recent traumatic event, much easier to recognize and identify, creating the symptoms of PTSD as in the case of combat veterans who were typical before going to war and become a different person when returning home. In either case, write all of it down on paper or on your computer. Interview others in your life, including loved ones and friends to sort out experiences when they happened. No matter how painful, revisit these incidents or events and make a record. Find the "hot buttons" that seem to surface as you revisit the past. Don't worry about your writing ability or the "spell-check" stuff. Do a brain dump and then go back and read it again to make revisions and fine tune the experience.

II. Personal Assessment

With all this information, sorted out and fine tuned, think about your own feelings and behavior. Start writing down how you feel and how the event(s) or experiences affected your behavior. Do you feel scared? Do you feel self doubt? Do you feel defensive? Do you feel shame? What kind of experiences do you have now that cause you to react in certain ways that could be considered negative in your own gut or what others say or how others react to you. Write all of this stuff down. Take a break and come back later and repeat this thinking process, and write some more. Take your time. Talk to loved ones and friends about this process and get their input. Write down all the input and thoughts from others. Go through this step over and over until you feel you have exhausted all the ideas and input.

III. Lessons Learned

In the final step, what have you learned from this exercise and process of self discovery? Write down short statements of what you learned or new awareness or discoveries about yourself that are concrete and objective. Take a break and come back later, and do this 3rd step until you feel all avenues of learning have been explored.

Now, see if you can identify some potential actions or solutions that might be helpful. If you can come up with just one action or solution this process is a win, win, win. Even if you don't realize the results right away, healing started with the first step of this process. It is very subtle but real. You are now ready to take action for on-going healing either on your own or with the assistance of professionals. Start engaging with loved ones and friends to share your findings. Reaching out is a key to success in healing.

The long term challenge of healing is the follow through and execution of self discovery actions. This is really where professionals can be the most help. But you have to do your homework to help someone professional to help you. You know the old saying, "help me help you."

References and Other Resources

http://www.history.navy.mil/faqs/stream/faq45-21.htm

http://ww2db.com/ship_spec.php?ship_id=99

http://www.lagunacounseling.com/

http://navy.togetherweserved.com/usn//voices/2011/23/Whitehouse_voices.html

http://www.ibiblio.org/hyperwar/USN/USN-ref.html

http://www.woundedwarriorproject.org/

http://unitedchildrenofveterans.com/

http://en.wikipedia.org/wiki/USS_Black_Hawk_(AD-9)

http://www.timemoneyandblood.com/HTML/shipsUSbattle/USStennessee.html

http://en.wikipedia.org/wiki/USS_Coucal_(ASR-8)

http://www.navsource.org/archives/10/12/1202.htm

http://www.ussbellegrove.com/

http://www.civilwarhome.com/macbio.htm

http://www.pearl-harbor.com/index.html

http://www.usswestvirginia.org/

http://www.pearlharborsurvivorsonline.org/html/events.htm

http://www.wvculture.org/history/usswv/usswv.html

http://www.sundrip.com/

http://www.wvculture.org/history/usswv/usswv.html

http://dutchschultz.blogspot.com/2007/03/how-ptsd-affects-veterans-children.html

http://en.wikipedia.org/wiki/X.25

http://www.neighborsforkids.org/

War Syndromes and Their Evaluation from the U.S. Civil War to the Present, Kenneth C. Hyams, Office of Public Health, Department of Veterans Affairs, Washington, DC. 2005.

About the Author

Steve Sparks is a retired information technology sales and marketing executive following over 35 years beginning with the US Navy as a radioman in 1963. He Graduated with a BA in Management from St. Mary's College, Moraga, California. Steve is married to his soul mate and business partner, Judy, and lives on the Oregon coast. He is the proud father of 3 grown daughters and 4 grandchildren and 1 great grandchild. In addition to writing, Steve's current passion and life work is mentoring and improving the education of K-12 kids, including helping the responsible non-profit agency www.neighborsforkids.org achieve sustainability.

CPSIA information can be obtained at www.ICGtesting.com
Printed in the USA
LVOW071055161012

303026LV00001B/16/P